"THOSE WHO PURSUE GREAT GOALS
DON'T REMEMBER PAST GRIEVANCES"
- EMPEROR GUANGWU

©2025 CATHERINE FET · NORTH LANDING BOOKS · ALL RIGHTS RESERVED

The history of China spans about 5,000 years. It's the longest continuous history of any nation in the world. For example, people who live in modern Egypt are not the same ethnic group that lived in Ancient Egypt. Modern Egyptians are Arabs who populated Egypt during the Islamic conquests of the 7th century. They speak Arabic, not Egyptian, they inherited none of the native Egyptian culture. The history of Ancient Egypt is not the history of today's Egypt. Unlike Egypt, China, which was invaded many times throughout its history and was ruled by foreign dynasties for centuries, absorbed all foreign influences, kept its native languages, its culture, and its national identity. It also swallowed the ancestral lands of its invaders, making them part of China! Out of 5,000 years of Chinese civilization, 3,500 years are "recorded history" – written down, in detail, in Chinese chronicles, government documents, and works of literature.

For many centuries China was far ahead of Europe in technology. Marco Polo, who traveled to China in the 13th century, marveled at the wide use of paper money, invented in China. Paper money came to Europe only in the 17th century. Back home in Venice, Marco Polo told people that the Chinese mined a kind of stone that was better fuel than wood – coal, still rare in Europe of that era. Gunpowder and firearms were invented in China in the 10th century, and arrived in Europe only 4 centuries later. Over 1000 years after the Chinese invention of paper (3rd century BC) Europeans were still writing their books and documents on animal skins, tree bark, papyrus, clay, wax... Europe adopted Chinese paper-making technology only in the 11th century.

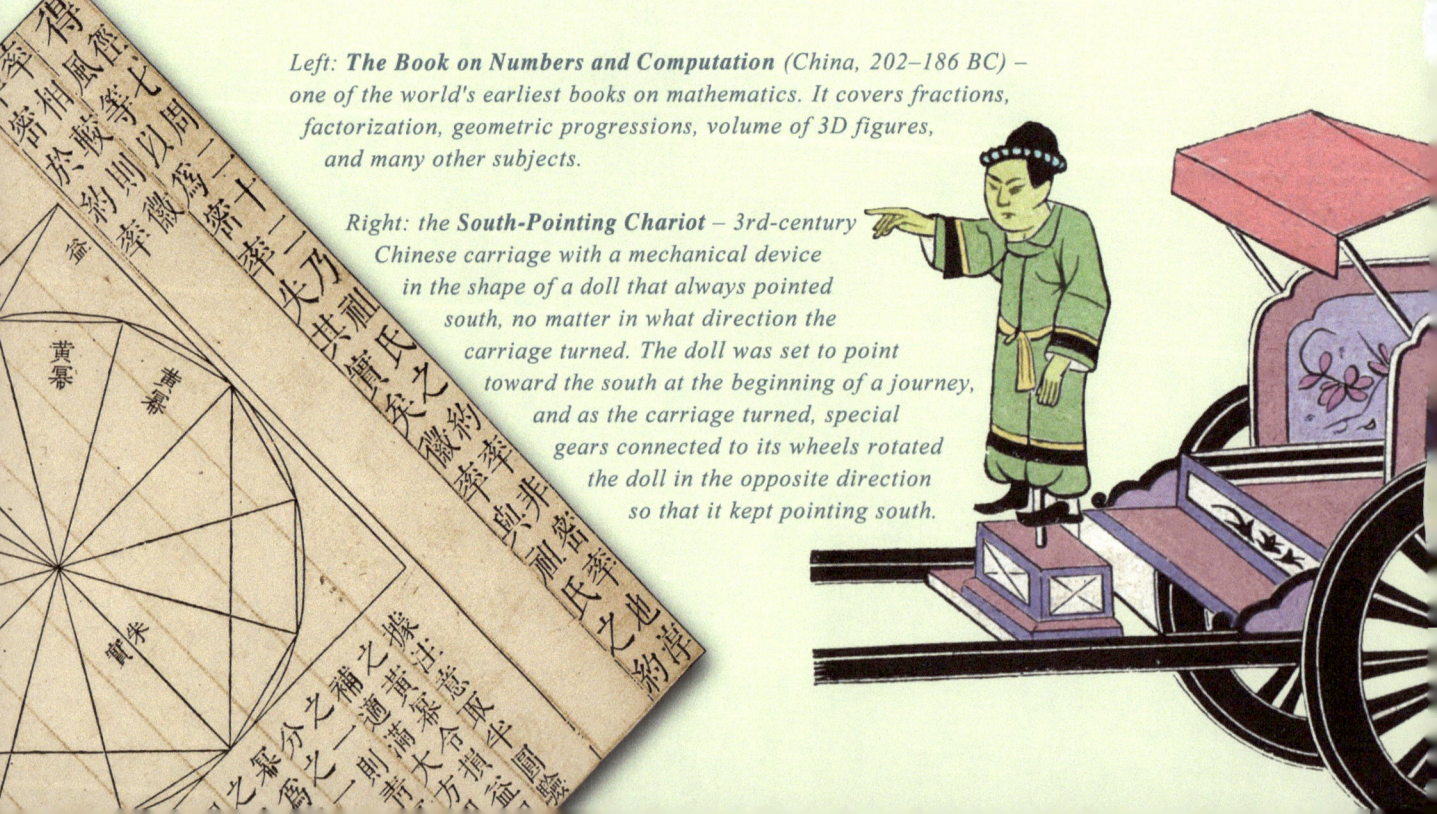

Left: **The Book on Numbers and Computation** (China, 202–186 BC) – one of the world's earliest books on mathematics. It covers fractions, factorization, geometric progressions, volume of 3D figures, and many other subjects.

Right: the **South-Pointing Chariot** – 3rd-century Chinese carriage with a mechanical device in the shape of a doll that always pointed south, no matter in what direction the carriage turned. The doll was set to point toward the south at the beginning of a journey, and as the carriage turned, special gears connected to its wheels rotated the doll in the opposite direction so that it kept pointing south.

Ancient China

Chinese history is usually taught as a sequence of 'dynasties' – the eras lasting from a few decades to a few centuries, during which China was ruled by this or that royal family. The earliest Chinese dynasty, Xia, was founded around 2070 BC, but everything we know about it comes from the Chinese historical texts collection *The Book of Documents* written 2000 years later. The Xia Dynasty was overthrown by the Shang Dynasty in 1600 BC. But, again, no written materials from that era survived except inscriptions on animal bones used for divination (predicting the future). The first dynasty that left us historical records was the Zhou dynasty (1046 - 256 BC) that replaced the Shang. In the 6th-5th centuries BC the great Chinese philosophers and political thinkers Lao Tsu and Confucius wrote down their systems of thought, and military strategist Sun Tzu created his masterpiece *The Art of War*. It's in this era that the earliest texts of *The Book of Documents* appeared. Since there are no historical records from the most ancient eras of Chinese history, the events of the Xia and Shang dynasties recorded in *The Book of Documents* are often viewed as legends. Many of the stories from that era are quite sensational! Here are some examples.

Yi Yin
From a slave to a prime minister, plus the story of a spy queen!

One day, in the 17th century BC, a slave woman went into the fields to collect some mulberry leaves. Out there she found an orphan kid, Yi Yin, and adopted him. Her husband, who worked as a cook in the kitchen of a noble wealthy family, taught the boy the art of making various delicacies, and, many years later, Yi Yin ended up working as a chef for Lord Tang – the powerful ruler of the State of Shang. As Yi Yin served meals to Lord Tang, Tang often talked to him, wondering if one day he could seize the throne from the hated Xia dynasty that ruled China. Unexpectedly, his chef offered him some brilliant advice. He came up with all sorts of ways to overthrow King Jie of the Xia dynasty. When Tang expressed his admiration for Yi Yin's strategic thinking, Yi Yin answered humbly that managing a kitchen wasn't much different from

Above: an 'Oracle bone' – an animal bone with a Chinese inscription used for divination, 1250 – 1050 BC

managing a country: There's an army of cooks, and a lot of drama – something is always boiling and running over. So, Yi Yin became the prime minister of the State of Shang, and with his help, Lord Tang bribed and recruited to his side the royal advisors of King Jie. More than that, Yi Yin turned the Xia queen, Mo Xi, into a spy! Queen Mo Xi loved luxury. Her palace was full of ivory, jade, and gold, but nothing amused her more than the sound made by expensive silk cloth when it was... torn! So her husband, the king, built a whole factory that wove silk day and night so the queen could destroy it all she wanted. However, more than silk, the queen desired to destroy her own husband, King Jie. Why? In her youth she had been a prisoner of war, captured from a noble clan defeated by King Jie. She never forgave the king the loss of her family, and eagerly agreed to spy on him for Yi Yin. Eventually, Yi Yin succeeded in uniting the clans dissatisfied with King Jie's rule. The army of Shang and its allies defeated King Jie. King Jie – together with Mo Xi! – were exiled to a faraway place somewhere in the mountains, and the new Shang dynasty was established. A brilliant political strategist, Yi Yin is also remembered as the "father of Chinese cuisine" (culinary art, art of cooking) and a skilled doctor. He is credited for inventing a number of herbal medicines used by Chinese doctors even today.

Jade

Jade is a semi-precious stone. In ancient China jade was more expensive than gold or silver. It was used to make jewelry, statues, and even palace walls. Powdered jade was added to food because many believed jade's magical power made one live a longer life. Below: An ancient Chinese burial "suit" made from jade. It was believed that jade could protect the body of a deceased person from decay.

Crazy King Zhou
and his scandalous lake of wine!

The last ruler of the Shang Dynasty, King Zhou of Shang (1105 BC – 1046 BC), is blamed for the downfall of his kingdom. He cared only about his own fun, and let his country slip out of his hands. The most scandalous reports of his reign are about his "pool of wine" and his "forest of meat." Zhou ordered the construction of a large pool and had it filled with... wine! In the middle of it was a tiny island, covered with trees, except the trees were artificial and their branches were skewers full of meat! The pool was large enough for a few small boats. So Zhou and his numerous wives spent all day drifting around the island, drinking wine from the pool and plucking meat off the "trees." To pay for the royal fun, the common people were burdened with enormous taxes. A rebellion was brewing, and some of the king's relatives and officials advised King Zhou to change his ways. So he had them all executed. When a rebel army showed up at the walls of his capital, Zhou piled all his treasures in a huge heap, climbed on top, set the pile on fire and perished in the flames. His pool of wine was destroyed, and why are we not surprised that the rebels banned alcohol in the kingdom? King Zhou was definitely bad news for his dynasty. However, some scholars believe that this history of the Shang dynasty may have been falsified (made false, distorted with lies) by later dynasties. It's totally likely that King Zhou of Shang was actually a normal boring king who never floated on a boat in a pool of wine.

Right & left: Cereal serving bowls, China, 10th century BC; Below: Spoon, China, 8th century BC

Spoiled Queen Bao Si
laughs at her husband's pranks as their kingdom falls apart!

King You of the Zhou dynasty ruled China in the 8th century BC. Like all Chinese kings, he had many wives, but his favorite queen was Bao Si. The problem was, Bao Si was easily bored, rarely laughed, and didn't seem to enjoy entertainment and celebrations at the court. Her gloomy depressive mood destroyed any fun King You tried to have. Having run out of ideas of how to amuse Bao Si, King You promised to pay a thousand ounces of gold to anyone in his kingdom and beyond who could make Bao Si laugh. Eager to earn the promised gold, one of King You's advisors suggested playing a prank on the rulers of China's northwestern provinces.

"Let's light the warning beacons on the mountain tops," he suggested. "The governors of the western provinces will think that we are being attacked by the **Quanrong** (nomadic tribes) and rush to the capital with their armies." The king thought it was a good idea. When the rulers of his provinces arrived in his palace with their troops – wearing armor, flying flags, and all ready for battle – gloomy Bao Si first giggled and then nearly fell out of her throne screaming with laughter. A few weeks later, the king repeated that "joke," and kept repeating it, until the governors rebelled and the entire Zhou kingdom collapsed.

LAO TSU AND TAOISM

Lao Tzu (6th-5th centuries BC) is one of the greatest Chinese philosophers and the founder of *Taoism*. Taoism comes from *Tao*, often translated as "the Way." The Tao is the force that shapes the universe, the universal order, and the path to personal enlightenment. Lao Tsu taught that to achieve harmony with the Tao, a person should live simply, following the rhythms of nature, and allowing events of one's life to unfold without resistance and struggle. Describing the essence of the universe, Lao Tzu used the idea of *yin and yang*, the unity of opposites. or example: Yin = dark, Yang = light; Yin = quiet, Yang = noise; Yin = female, Yang = male. Lao Tzu taught his students to seek balance in life and inner peace – the state of harmony with oneself and the world.

"Lao Tsu on his buffalo followed by a disciple" by a Chinese artist, 19th century; Right: Yin and Yang symbol

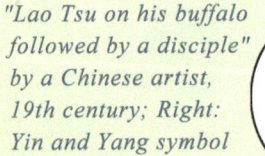

Lao Tzu worked as a historian and the librarian of the capital of the Zhou Kingdom. At some point the country was shaken by riots and political struggle, and Lao Tzu decided to leave looking for a quieter place. But on the border of the kingdom, a border guard recognized him and asked Lao Tzu to write down his teaching, so that people of his country could study it after the great teacher left. Lao Tzu agreed, wrote down his ideas, handed the manuscript to the border guard, and was gone, never to be seen again.

Short sword with ornate handle, China 6th-5th centuries BC

CONFUCIUS AND CONFUCIANISM

Confucius (551 – 479 BC) was a Chinese philosopher and political thinker whose teaching on moral values, social harmony, and the importance of education profoundly influenced Chinese culture, government, and family traditions. His philosophy, *Confucianism*, prioritizes • respect for the wisdom of the older members of families and society • being responsible for one's actions • self-improvement • and maintaining peace and social order by making decisions based on good judgement and compassion.

Confucius' dad was a military officer who traced his family to the Shang dynasty, but he died when Confucius was 3, so Confucius was raised by his mom, in poverty. As a kid he studied the Six Arts – a typical public school curriculum of the Zhou Dynasty era: Rituals (civil and religious), Music, Archery, Horseback (and chariot) Riding, Calligraphy (writing) and Literature, and Math. As a grownup he worked as a bookkeeper, and held various positions in the local government of his native State of Lu. Confucius became famous as a teacher and was appointed the governor of a town. When political struggle between different noblemen's clans resulted in riots and war, Confucius fled from his homeland. After many hardships, and years in exile, he came back, invited by the government of the State of Lu. Confucius was married and had 3 kids. He admired Lao Tsu and traveled to visit him. Here are some of the most-quoted sayings by Confucius:

- Wherever you go, go with all your heart.
- It does not matter how slowly you go, as long as you don't stop.
- In a country well governed, poverty is something to be ashamed of.
  In a country badly governed, wealth is something to be ashamed of.
- Success is not never falling, but rising every time you fall.
- Respect yourself, and others will respect you.
- Better a diamond with a flaw than a perfect pebble.
- If you want to shape the future, study the past.
- He who learns, but doesn't think for himself, will perish.
  He who thinks for himself, but never learns, is in great danger as well.

DURING THE LIFETIME OF CONFUCIUS:

- The founder of Buddhism, Siddhartha Gautama, known as the Buddha, lived in ancient India.
- In the 540s BC The Babylonian empire fell, and King Cyrus the Great founded the Persian Empire. In 535 BC he led the first Persian invasion of the Indus Valley. In 525 BC the Persians conquered Egypt, and King Darius of Persia linked the Nile and the Red Sea by building a canal.
- In 510 BC Ancient Greek philosopher and mathematician Pythagoras established his school.
- In 510 BC Ancient Rome overthrew its king, Tarquinius Superbus, and became a republic.
- In 490 King Darius of Persia attacked Greece, but lost the Battle of Marathon. Phidippides ran 40 kilometers from Marathon to Athens with the news of the Greek victory.
- In 480 Ancient Greek King Leonidas of Sparta and 300 of his soldiers took their last stand in the Battle of Thermopylae to allow the Greeks escape the Persian army commanded by Darius' son, King Xerxes.

Sun Tzu

Sun Tzu (544 – 496 BC) was a military commander in the Chinese State of Wu. He is considered one of the greatest military strategists in history thanks to his book *The Art of War* – a collection of ideas on managing military conflicts and winning battles. At the end of the 6th century the power of the Zhou dynasty declined, while the population grew, and China entered a period of endless infighting between its many provinces and independent states.

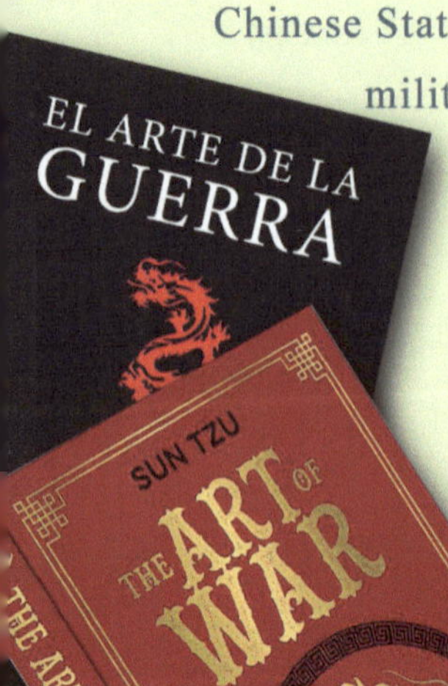

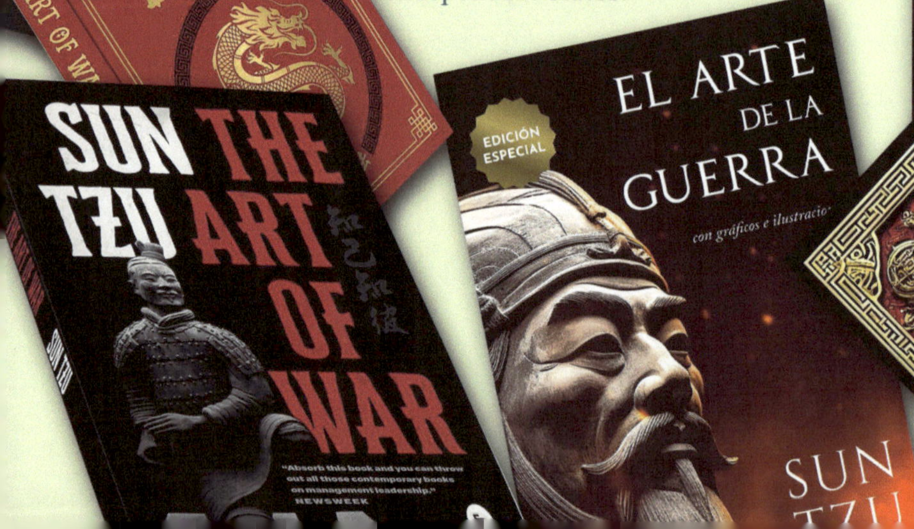

Chinese rulers sought talented military advisors to help them both win battles and avoid wars with stronger neighbors. Here are a few ideas from Sun Tzu's masterpiece, *The Art of War*. They seem obvious, but, remember, Sun Tzu was the first in history to write down such ideas. It was the beginning of military theory.

- It's best to win without going to war. Countries facing a military conflict should use *diplomacy* and deception to trick and corner their enemy and prevent all-out war.
- The ruler of the state must provide moral leadership and explain to his people why their cause is just and worth fighting and dying for.
- The key to winning a war is collecting *intelligence* on the enemy. Recruiting spies and gathering information about the enemy's strengths and weaknesses is vital to achieving victory.
- Deception is an important weapon of war. Feeding the enemy *misinformation* about your capabilities tricks them into making blunders. *Psychological warfare* is a form of deception. If you convince your enemy that they are weaker than you and are likely to lose, the war is half-won.
- The *morale* of the troops – their sense of motivation and faith in victory – is the factor that will decide the outcome of any battle.

Sun Tzu led the army of Wu to many victories. For example, with 30,000 well-trained soldiers he defeated the army of the Chu kingdom that numbered 200,000. Nevertheless, his enemies kept whispering behind his back that he was better at writing than at putting his military theories into practice. One day the king of Wu decided to have fun at Sun Tzu's expense and ordered him to give military training to his numerous wives and female servants at the palace, and turn them into a real military unit. Sun Tzu appointed two of the king's favorite wives "unit commanders" and said they would be responsible for their "soldiers" carrying out the orders. However, when the women heard military commands, such as "turn right" or "turn left," they giggled and refused to obey. Then Sun Tzu ordered the execution of the unit "commanders" – the king's favorite wives. The king protested, but Sun Tzu insisted that if soldiers refused to follow orders, there was only one way to deal with the problem – execute their immediate commanders. So the two favorite king's wives were put to death. After that the "unit" followed the orders flawlessly and nobody dared to laugh at Sun Tzu again.

Qin Shi Huang
259 – 210 BC

Qin Shi Huang was the 1st emperor of China and the founder of the Qin (pronounced as "chin") Dynasty. The word 'China' comes from the name of this dynasty. Qin Shi Huang's birth name was Ying Zheng. In 246 BC, when his dad, the king of Qin died, Ying Zheng was only 13. Right away, he faced powerful enemies at the royal court. His mom, Lady Zhao, the Empress Dowager (*dowager* = a royal widow) found herself a new boyfriend and had two babies with him. The boyfriend, behind the empress' back, was planning to overthrow Ying Zheng and replace him with one of his own kids. Even worse, Ying Zheng's official guardian, the royal prime minister Lu Buwei, was on the side of the conspirators. And as if that wasn't enough, the kingdom of Qin was at war with 6 other Chinese kingdoms – Han, Zhao, Wei, Chu, Yan, and Qi. No wonder this time was called the **Warring States Period** (403 – 221 BC).

In 235 BC Lady Zhao's boyfriend stole her royal seal and used it to issue orders to the Qin army to march on the kingdom's capital Xianyang (pronounced 'she-an-yang'). But the young King Ying Zheng, who by that time had turned 21, offered 1 million copper coins for the head of his mom's boyfriend and mobilized military commanders loyal to the throne to put down the rebellion. The enemies were defeated. Lady Zhao's boyfriend and all his family were captured and executed "to the 3rd degree" (meaning, himself, his parents, and his grandparents), and the royal guardian Lu Buwei was politely advised to drink a cup of poisoned wine, which he did.

Next, Ying Zheng led his army against the 6 enemy "warring states" and conquered them all. In 221 BC he became the first ruler of a unified China. The title 'king' didn't seem grand enough to honor this achievement, so he chose the title 'emperor.' Qin Shi Huang = Qin (Qin dynasty) Shi (first) Huang (emperor). All the soldiers of the former "warring states" were joined into a new imperial army. To ensure that his generals received orders directly from him and from nobody else, Qin Shi Huang gave each commander a "tiger tally" – half of a little tiger figurine. The generals accepted the orders only if a messenger who delivered them brought with him the other, matching half of the tally.

Qin Shi Huang decreed that the same *currency* (money) be used throughout China. The coins had holes in them so that they could be carried on a string. Weights and measures used in business, manufacturing, and construction were *standardized* (made standard – the same throughout the land). The distance between the wheels of carriages was standardized too. What for? Carriage wheels made ruts (tracks) in the dirt roads. Carriages with the same distance between the wheels could travel in the same ruts where the wheels that rolled there before them had already pounded the dirt into solid dry tracks. Qin Shi Huang ordered the defensive fortifications between the former "warring states" be demolished and wide roads be built between their capitals. To defend the northern borders of the empire from attack by the nomadic *Xiongnu* tribes, hundreds of thousands of workers were gathered to join the defensive walls of the Qin, Zhao and Yan states from west to east. That was the earliest portion of the *Great Wall of China*! The writing system of the state of Qin became the official Chinese writing system, strictly enforced throughout the empire. The characters were simplified and their number was reduced to about 3,000.

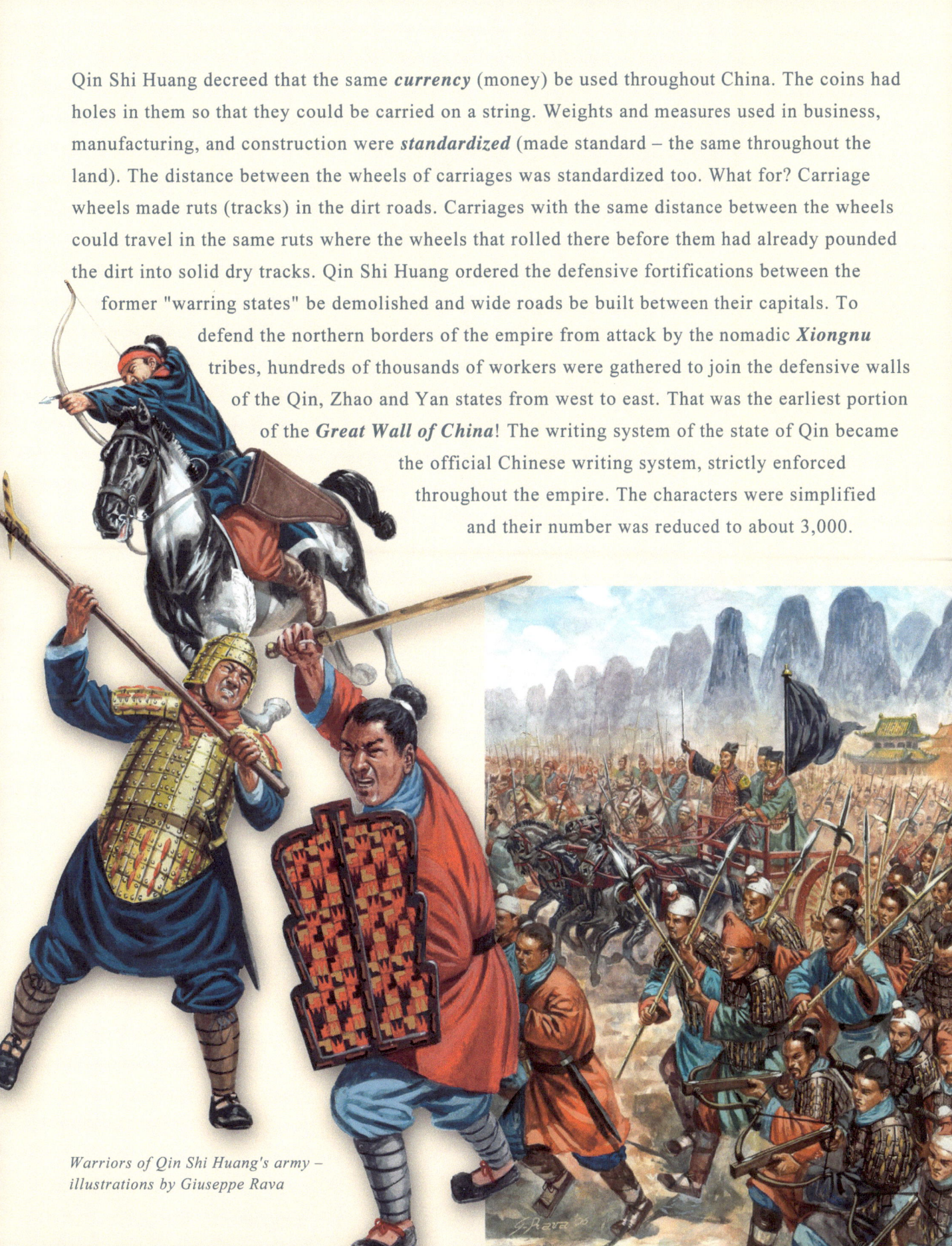

Warriors of Qin Shi Huang's army – illustrations by Giuseppe Rava

Chinese writing

Many Chinese characters evolved from **pictographs** – pictures of objects or symbols standing for ideas. Each character stands either for a word, or for a portion of a word (like a prefix or a suffix) with its own meaning. To read and write in Chinese a person needs to memorize thousands of characters. College-educated Chinese speakers remember about 4,000 characters. Examples of Chinese characters and their pronunciation in **Mandarin Chinese**: 人 (ren – 'person'), 日 (ri – 'sun'), 上 (shang – 'up'), 下 (xia – 'down'), 木 (mu – 'tree'), 三 (san – 'three'). Chinese characters contain no hint of how to pronounce them. You can read them in any language!

While the Chinese kings of previous eras surrounded themselves with noble families who inherited their titles and land from previous generations, Qin Shi Huang erased and "restarted" this *feudal system* by granting land to talented people of any origin or status in return for loyal service. In Xianyang he built copies of the royal palaces from each state he defeated – as a symbol of his authority over the whole of China. Next he forced the royal families of the former "warring states" to move into these palaces. Keeping them in the capital, under the watchful eye of Qin Shi Huang's government, made it less likely that they would rebel. These royal families, however, didn't give up hope of freeing themselves from Qin Shi Huang's grip. One day the royal family of Yan plotted to *assassinate* (murder) the emperor. They hired an assassin who wrapped a dagger dipped in poison in a paper map and showed up at the royal palace asking to see the emperor. He said he had come from the state of Yan bringing presents as a token of good will – the map and the head of one of the Qin generals killed in battle. When the assassin unwrapped the map in front of Qin Shi Huang and pulled out the dagger, the emperor was left to defend himself on his own, because his guards and court officials were not allowed to carry weapons in the royal palace! The assassin tried to stab Qin Shi Huang, but the emperor pulled his own sword and wounded the assassin! Then the assassin threw the dagger at him, but missed, and was finally seized by the panic-stricken palace guards.

But that wasn't the end of the assassination plot. Another man loyal to the royal Yan family decided to try his luck at killing the emperor – Gao Jianli, a famous musician who played *zhu*, an ancient Chinese string instrument. One day Gao Jianli was invited to play for Qin Shi Huang at the royal palace. He attached a slab of lead to the wooden body of his instrument and was planning to smash the emperor's head with it. However, when he entered the palace, one of the guards recognized him and figured out his plan. The emperor didn't want to kill such a famous musician, so he ordered to blind him. Once Gao Jianli's eyes were put out, the emperor ordered him to play music. In the middle of his performance blind Gao Jianli stopped and rushed in the direction where he had heard Qin Shi Huang's voice, swinging his lead-weighted zhu. He was seized and executed.

Feudal, Feudalism

Feudalism is a social system in which **aristocracy** (lords, noble families) receive land from a king in exchange for providing troops to defend their country and the royal family. The nobles distribute this land to their **vassals** – tenants. Vassals serve in the nobles' military units and pay them for the use of the land. The vassals collect a share of the produce or money from peasants, craftsmen, and merchants who live and work on their land in exchange for military protection.

'Feudal' comes from the Medieval Latin 'feudum' – land granted in exchange for service. It is not related to the word 'feud' (hostilities) which comes from the Old English 'fede' – 'war.' "Vassal" comes from the Old French word meaning 'servant.'

Did the Great Wall of China provide an effective defense against invasions?

The Great Wall of China is 13,170 miles (21,196 km) long. It was built from earth, stone, wood, and, later, bricks. It was not built to seal the Western border of China, but to stop or slow down the raids by the nomadic tribes from the steppes of Mongolia. To get their horsemen to the other side of the wall the enemy had to breach it, or build ramps to get the horses over it – both practically impossible for nomads with no engineering expertise or wall-breaking machinery. The wall was also an obstacle for potential raiders on their way back – transporting plunder, prisoners, and captured herds of cattle across the wall was impossible. There were gates, but they were defended by strong Chinese garrisons.

To prevent wars, the emperor collected all the weapons from every former "warring state" – with the exception of those that belonged to his own army – and had them melted and cast into giant copper statues and bells. Realizing that many books and documents written in the "warring states" promoted hatred against their neighbors, Qin Shi Huang ordered the burning of books – all books written before China was unified, except books on medicine, alchemy, farming, and the history of Qin. Two copies of each book to be burned were preserved in the imperial libraries. The royal book-burning decree also stated, "Anyone who uses history to criticize the present shall have his family executed... Anyone who has failed to burn the books after thirty days of this announcement shall be subjected to tattooing and be sent to build the Great Wall." The types of books the emperor considered most dangerous and most likely to spread anti-government ideas were collections of poetry, historical chronicles, and books on philosophy. Some scholars refused to give their books away for the burning and were promptly shipped off to build the Great Wall.

In his 40s Qin Shi Huang became very **superstitious**. He believed in all sorts of evil **omens** (signs), spirits and ghosts, and built tunnels from his main palace to 270 other palaces and houses so he could travel between them underground where, he hoped, the evil forces wouldn't see him. Terrified of assassins, he slept in a different palace each night! Qin Shi Huang was also obsessed with the "elixir of life" – a legendary medicine capable of extending a person's life or maybe even making one immortal. Some **alchemists** swore they had a recipe for the elixir of life and claimed they had already achieved immortality. But there was no proof whether they were mortal or immortal, until it occurred to Qin Shi Huang to bury some of them alive along with the book-burning protesters – to test if their claim was true. Legend has it that he buried alive two alchemists who had sold him fake "elixir of life" plus 460 other scholars he suspected of disapproving his policies. His oldest son, Fusu, dared to ask his dad not to kill scholars, and was sent to guard the empire's northern borders as punishment.

In search of the "elixir of life," Qin Shi Huang also sent an expedition on multiple ships to look for Mount Penglai described in Chinese mythology as the place populated with the immortal beings. The expedition never returned. Legends said that the sailors had never found Mount Penglai, but, since their mission failed, they were afraid to go back to China, and settled in Japan.

"The burning of the books" by James William Giles

In 211 a meteor fell down in Qin, in the town of Dongjun. And by the time it was reached by local authorities, someone had left an inscription on a rock nearby: "The First Emperor will die and his land will be divided." None of the Dongjun residents admitted to having written these words, so Qin Shi Huang ordered the whole population of that town executed. The prophecy, however, came true. The following year, while traveling in Shadong province in search of the "elixir of life," Qin Shi Huang died. He was 49, and it was unclear whether he died of illness or poison. Some guessed he had been killed by **mercury** in one of the "elixirs of life" sold to him by alchemists. The royal officials were afraid to announce the emperor's death. So, while carrying his body to Xianyang, they pretended they were serving him meals, washing his clothes and writing down his orders. Meanwhile, his body started decomposing in the summer heat, and, to conceal the smell of death, they pulled a cart of smelly fish in front of his carriage.

Shortly before his death Qin Shi Huang wrote a letter to his oldest son, Fusu, making him the heir to the throne. He asked the tutor of his youngest son, Huhai, to deliver the letter. But the tutor disliked Fusu. He wanted Huhai on the throne. He threw away the emperor's letter and *forged* (faked) another one, ordering Fusu to kill himself as a punishment for some blunders mentioned in the fake letter. Fusu, who never questioned his father's orders, took his own life, and Huhai ascended the throne. His first order of business was to kill all of his dad's wives and all of his siblings. However, several years later peasant riots and nobles' revolts shook the empire, and it fell apart. In 207 BC, thinking that the royal palace was under attack by rebels, Huhai killed himself, and several years later rebel leader Liu Bang, born to a peasant family, came to power and founded the Han Dynasty that gave its name to the *Han* people – the largest ethnic group in China.

Alchemy

In the ancient world and all the way to the 18th century alchemy was believed to be the art of manipulating substances to achieve magical results. Alchemists conducted chemical and physical experiments trying to turn various metals into gold, or to create magical potions and elixirs. Alchemy was a mix of science and magic. The word 'alchemy' comes from the Arabic 'al' = 'the' and 'khemia,' the word that referred to the magical arts of Egypt, because of the ancient name for Egypt – Khem ("black earth"). This is where our word 'chemistry' comes from. Because many sciences, such as chemistry, physics, and medicine came from alchemy, alchemists called their art "The Mother of all Science and Wisdom."

Chinese Superstitions

Superstition is belief in supernatural influences that, supposedly, lead to either good or bad luck and various positive or negative events in a person's life. For example, in China the number 8 is considered lucky, while the number 4 is unlucky. Many buildings in China don't have a 4th floor. They call it the 5th floor instead, and the evil spirits have never been able to figure out this clever trick! Many Chinese believe that the color white brings bad luck because it's worn at funerals. Red is the color of good fortune and protection from evil spirits. They also believe that doors facing south bring good luck and fortune, while doors that face north invite evil spirits. So if you live on the 4th floor with your door facing north, like me – watch out!

The Terracotta army

Around 246 BC, when 13-year-old Qin Shi Huang became king of Qin, he started building a massive tomb for himself. Continuing for decades, this project employed over 700,000 workers and was never finished. Underground areas of the tomb were filled with life-sized **terracotta** statues – 8,000 warriors, 130 chariots with 520 horses – which were supposed to come to life and protect the emperor after his death. Plus there are some statues of government officials, circus performers, and musicians. **Terracotta** ("baked earth" in Italian) is made from clay fired (hardened in fire) into a ceramic substance. The **Terracotta Army** was only discovered in 1974 by farmers digging a well in the Shaanxi province of China. After more than 2000 years underground, the clay figures were well preserved. The only element that didn't survive is the paint that covered the terracotta figures. Most of it peeled off. The pigments in the paint were made from ground minerals and semi-precious stones– malachite (green), azurite (blue), charcoal (black), iron oxide (dark red), and others.

ZHANG QIAN

2nd century BC

The Han dynasty (206 BC – AD 220) is often called "the Golden Age" of ancient China. During that era, Confucianism became the official religion of the empire, and the *Silk Road* – the famous trade route from China to Europe and Africa was established. The Silk Road ran through China, Central Asia, Afghanistan, India, Iran, Iraq, Syria, Turkey, and reached Rome. The explorer and diplomat who made the trade along the Silk Road possible by mapping its route was Zhang Qian (pronounced 'jang chee-an').

In 140 BC, Emperor Wu ascended the throne of the Han Dynasty. As his top priority he set the war against the nomadic *Xiongnu* tribes (pronounced 'zaang-noo,' 'children of slaves' in Chinese) who kept raiding Chinese lands along the Western border of China. Emperor Wu wanted to open trade routes to Central Asia and make travel safe. His allies in this mission were the Yuezhi tribes in the *steppes* (grasslands) of the "Western Regions" (Central Asia) who also suffered from the the Xiongnu attacks. The Xiongnu had killed the Yuezhi king and turned his skull into a wine cup. The Yuezhi royal family wanted revenge. Emperor Wu recruited 99 Chinese diplomats and soldiers to travel to the lands of the Yuezhi (in present-day Tajikistan), help them organize defense against the Xiongnu, and map their territory. Zhang Qian led that expedition. He took along with him a guide, named Ganfu who had been a Xiongnu prisoner of war.

Chinese Names

*In Chinese names the family name (= surname) usually goes first, followed by the given name. So Chinese "last names" are actually first names! For example, Zhang Qian came from the Zhang family. Like Western names, Chinese family names are **patrilineal** (from Latin 'pater' = father + 'līnea' = a line) – kids inherit names from their fathers, not their mothers.*

The expedition traveled hundreds of miles, hiding by day and marching by night. They crossed the Yellow River unnoticed, but got lost in the desert – and were captured by the Xiongnu!

Statue of Zhang Qian in Hanzhong, China

Years passed. Zhang Qian and Ganfu lived as slaves in Xiongnu captivity, guarding herds of sheep. Over time Zhang Qian gained the respect and trust of the Xiongnu ruler and was offered a Xiongnu bride. He married and had a son. But he never forgot or abandoned his mission. All the while he worked on his maps and looked for an opportunity to escape. 13 years after Zhang Qian became a prisoner of the Xiongnu, he arranged an escape for himself, Ganfu, his wife and kid. They traveled for weeks, hiding in the mountains and deserts of what is today the Xinjiang province of China, until they made their way to the Yuezhi. But times had changed, and the Yuezhi were no longer willing to fight the Xiongnu. Having spent a year with the Yuezhi, Zhang Qian, his family, and Ganfu left. They headed home toward China, but on their way they were once again captured by the Xiongnu.

The Xiongnu ruler, impressed with Zhang Qian's courage and his loyalty to China, promised not to bother him as long as he stayed as a prisoner in the Xiongnu camp. But two years later the ruler died and the Xiongnu Confederacy was ripped apart by riots and infighting. Zhang Qian and his companions took advantage of the chaos among the Xiongnu and escaped to Han territory: China! Zhang Qian came home in 125 BC bringing Emperor Wu accurate detailed maps of the "Western Regions" and descriptions of the cultures and lifestyles of the peoples inhabiting them. Emperor Wu granted Zhang Qian the title of royal counsellor and used this information to take military action against the Xiongnu, driving them further away from the Chinese borders.

Zhang Qian always traveled carrying a bamboo pole with 3 bundles of ox hair – an emblem of his mission as a Chinese diplomat; Right: a statue of Zhang Qian at the Shaanxi Museum; Below: Mountains in Xinjiang, Chinese Central Asia

Silk and Sericulture

Silk is protein fiber produced by silkworms to form the *cocoons* they spin around themselves to protect themselves as they grow into a moth. The best silk comes from the Silk Moth that feeds on mulberry leaves. Silk protein molecules form structures similar to triangular *prisms*. These prisms *refract* (break the direction of) the light and *reflect* it at different angles – giving silk its beautiful shine! Breaking out of its cocoon, the moth bites its way through the silk fiber, tearing it. To preserve the fiber intact so it could be un-spun into long threads, the silkworms have to be killed while still inside the cocoon. Once this technique was discovered, the *sericulture* – cultivation of silkworms – began. The ancient Chinese people started cultivating silkworms and producing silk in the 4th-3rd millennium BC, but silk reached the West only after the Silk Road became an established trade route.

In 53 BC the Romans suffered one of the greatest defeats in their history. It is said they lost the Battle of Carrhae to the Persians after the Persians unfurled their banners. Made of Chinese silk and shining like fire in the blazing sun, these astonishing banners broke the fighting spirit of the Romans. In AD14 the price of silk in Rome was higher than that of gold. Europeans were desperate to find out the secret of silk. But Chinese emperors prohibited taking silkworms beyond China's borders. Border guards searched every traveler.

One legend has it that the secret of silk was smuggled out of China by a Chinese princess traveling to the Kingdom of Khotan (present-day northwest China) to marry its ruler. Unwilling to live the rest of her life without silk dresses, the princess hid the silkworms and mulberry seeds in her crown! Even though Persia was the center of the silk trade in the West, the Persians started cultivating silkworms only around the 6th century. From Persia, sericulture was brought to Constantinople, the capital of Byzantium – the Eastern Roman Empire. Italy began manufacturing silk fabrics only in the middle of the 12th century, after King Roger II of Sicily captured 2000 silk spinning workers from Byzantium during the Second Crusade and brought them to Italy.

WANG MANG
45 BC – AD 23

In 9 AD a man by the name of Wang Mang **usurped** (seized) the Han Dynasty throne. Who was Wang Mang? He was a court official and a relative of the royal family. Unlike his royal relatives he didn't waste money on luxuries and entertainment. Instead of richly-embroidered silk outfits, Wang Mang wore simple clothes of a Confucian scholar. Wang Mang's cousin, Han Emperor Cheng didn't seem to notice that his government officials competed in corruption, causing peasant riots to flare up again and again across the empire. All his attention was consumed by the intrigues inside his own palace. Emperor Cheng fell in love with two dancers who performed at his court, the Zhao sisters. The sisters accused Emperor Cheng's wife, the empress, of witchcraft, convinced him to kick his wife out of his court and marry both of them.

To secure a chance for their own kids to inherit the throne, the Zhao sisters murdered the only two sons born to the emperor – both still babies. One was starved to death and the other died in prison. Even worse, it was rumored that Emperor Cheng knew about the sisters' conspiracy against his kids and didn't stop them. He spent fortunes building and decorating lavish palaces for the Zhao sisters. Here is a description of the evil sisters' home from historical chronicles called *The Book of Han*: "The atrium of their palace was painted entirely scarlet red, while the bedrooms were painted black. The thresholds were made of copper, and were covered with gold. Each step of the staircases was carved from white jade, and the walls were trimmed with solid gold. The palace was decorated with jade and pearls. Ever since there were imperial palaces, there had never been one so luxurious." However, neither the Zhao sisters, nor any other of Emperor Cheng's wives gave birth to boys, and, when the emperor died in 7 BC, there was no heir to the Han throne. That opened the door for other members of the royal family to compete for the crown. Cheng's cousin, Emperor Ai won the crown. Wang Mang, who was a military commander at that time, supported the new emperor but soon got himself into major trouble with the royal family.

Back of a bronze mirror, China 1st-2nd century

Once at a royal banquet he noticed that the seat for Emperor Ai's grandmother was placed right next to that of Emperor Cheng's grandmother, Empress Dowager Wang. Both grandmothers had once been married to the same man, Emperor Yuan, but while Cheng's grandmother had been the empress, Ai's grandmother had been just a low-ranking wife. So Wang Mang moved Ai's grandma's seat to a less prestigious place. For that he was expelled from the imperial court into exile. But Emperor Cheng's grandmother, Empress Dowager Wang, appreciated that Wang Mang protected her status, and 6 years later, when Emperor Ai died leaving no heir to the throne, she called Wang Mang back from exile and appointed him the head of the imperial government. The throne was given to Empress Wang's 8-year-old stepson who was crowned Emperor Ping. Wang Mang convinced the empress to prohibit Ping's mom from ever visiting her kid in the royal palace. He didn't want to share power and influence with yet another bunch of royal relatives!

Now, having nearly unlimited authority over the Han Empire, Wang Mang went after his enemies. One of the surviving evil Zhao sisters and Ai's wife were stripped of all their titles and properties and ordered to guard the tombs of their husbands. Ai's grandma, who had died by that time, was dug out of her grave and stripped of the jade jewelry that adorned her corpse. She was shipped to be reburied somewhere faraway and her grave was covered with thorns! Wang Mang also started working on his own path toward the imperial crown. He bribed a tribe in Southern China to bring to the royal court a rare white pheasant they had caught, and announce it was a sign that a new emperor (Wang Mang, of course) was coming to create a new dynasty. Next, Wang Mang decided to have his daughter marry the child emperor Ping. "It's time to find a bride for Emperor Ping," he declared, and, with fake modesty, he asked that his own daughter be not considered as a potential bride. Next, he gathered a crowd of his supporters and directed them to surround the palace of the old Empress Wang demanding that Emperor Ping marry Wang Mang's daughter. Stunned with such an outpouring of love for Wang Mang, the old empress agreed and Wang Mang's daughter became empress!

Meanwhile out there, in the towns and villages of China, Wang Mang was, indeed, much loved and respected by the common people.

"Knife" and "spade" Chinese coins issued duing the reign of Wang Mang

He introduced new rules at the court that prohibited wealthy noblemen from wasting their money on luxury and ordered them to live modestly and donate money to help the poor. He made dozens of aristocrats donate land on which he built tens of thousands of houses to be given – for free – to people who lost homes in floods and fires. He summoned the best scholars from all around China to the capital and had them give free classes to common people. As a reward each scholar was given a house.

In 5 BC Emperor Ping turned 13 and told Wang Mang what he really thought about him. So Wang Mang served him some poisoned wine. Once the emperor died, Wang Mang put some 1-year-old kid from the royal family on the throne and declared himself the "acting emperor." Three years later Wang Mang's supporters found a stone tablet with an "ancient prophecy" stating that Wang Mang would rise to be the emperor by the will of the gods. And, as the final argument, Wang Mang claimed a stone statue of an ancient saint had talked to him and asked him to guide China through troubled times... How could he say no to a talking statue? Wang Mang seized the throne, announced a new dynasty – Xin (pronounced 'shin') – and initiated a series of reforms that were truly revolutionary.

- Wang Mang abolished slavery, and made the slave trade illegal.
- He *nationalized* all farmland in China (made it the property of the state, not private property).

Chinese Calligraphy

Calligraphy is decorative writing with a pen or brush. It's an art form. A word, a saying, or a poem hand-written in a beautiful script becomes a work of visual art similar to a painting. The style of writing – stroke variations, color intensity, width of the line, and distance between the characters – expresses emotion and adds to the meaning of the written text.

- Large landowners were ordered to distribute some of their land for free among farmers. Anyone could receive farmland for free. The size of the land given to each family depended on the number of their family members.
- The poor could receive a house for free, or get a *loan* (borrow money) from the government with little or no *interest* (payment for the loan).
- The salaries of government officials were increased or decreased depending on how much money was collected in taxes for the imperial treasury.
- Wang Mang undermined the power of wealthy merchants by establishing a state *monopoly* (control) on the production of salt, iron, and alcohol.
- Wang Mang was the first to introduce an *income tax* in China. Every citizen had to pay 10% of their earnings to the state. Everyone had to work and pay taxes. Anyone who didn't have a job had to either pay a "laziness tax" or work on government projects.

The "laziness tax" was Wang Mang's favorite idea. He believed that any problem could be solved with hard work. He worked every night, all night long, and often fell asleep at his desk during the day as his advisors and military commanders delivered their reports. Most of Wang Mang's reforms turned disastrous – even for the poor people to whom these reforms were supposed to bring relief. Government officials quickly got used to taking bribes from landowners and wealthy families, and *sabotaged* (obstructed) Wang Mang's reforms. So much government money was wasted or stolen that Wang Mang created a secret police that spied on every government official. But the police took bribes too! The number of orders he issued was insane, and most of them were never carried out. Eventually the royal families ruling China's provinces organized uprisings seeking to split away. Peasant riots erupted again.

One of the farmers' riots was led by the Liu brothers – Liu Yan and Liu Xiu (pronounced 'lee-oo shee-oo') – distant relatives of the royal Han dynasty. Their dad had been a governor of a small town, but he died early and his kids were raised by their uncle, a farmer, working in the fields. When the Liu brothers joined the rebels, they didn't have enough money to buy two war horses. So the younger brother, Liu Xiu – the future Han emperor – rode into his first battle on the back of a cow! Instead of just raiding the enemy camps and burning crops, the Liu brothers tried to capture and hold as much territory as they could, growing their army and the "country" they controlled. Many rebel groups, including other members of the Liu family, joined them, believing that they would bring back the Han dynasty. But when it came to choosing one of the rebel leaders as the new Han Dynasty emperor, the Liu clan, jealous of the Liu brothers' fame, chose their third cousin, Liu Xuan (pronounced 'lee-oo soo-an') and "crowned" him emperor.

Having won a number of battles against Wang Mang's army, Liu Xiu led the rebels to the empire's capital. Wang Mang knew that his days were numbered. He sat in his palace testing magic spells with a couple alchemists who promised to defeat his enemies with witchcraft. His military commanders suspected Wang Mang had gone insane, because he started addressing them with strange titles like, "The Colonel Holding a Great Axe to Chop Down Withered Wood." When the rebels attacked and broke down the palace doors, Wang Mang hid in a high tower in the middle of a lake. His guards fought to the end, retreating up the stairs of the tower, step-by-step, until the rebels found and killed Wang Mang. So many rebel warriors claimed they were the one who killed Wang Mang, that his body was cut into small pieces, and only his head was delivered to Liu Xiu.

Emperor Guangwu
5 BC – AD 57

While Liu Xiu fought against Wang Mang, his cousin, the "emperor," envious of the Liu brothers' popularity, assassinated Liu Xiu's brother, Liu Yan. Then, scared of Liu Xiu's revenge, the "emperor" gave Liu Xiu the title of the "Great General Smashing the Enemy" and appointed him Minister of War.

Liu Xiu seemed to behave as if nothing happened, never betraying his anger. He fulfilled his government duties... he married a girl with whom he had fallen in love as a teenager. A few months after his wedding, Liu Xuan ordered him to go to the leaders of a farmers' revolt north of the Yellow River and demand that they surrender. Liu Xiu knew that he was being sent on a suicide mission, but he had a plan of his own. He sent his wife, Yin Lihua, to live with her parents, and headed for the Yellow River. Instead of negotiating with the rebel warlords on behalf of the "emperor," Liu Xiu made friends with them and organized their forces into his own private army – well-trained and well-armed. He also started replacing local government officials with his own supporters. One of the rebel warlords asked Liu Xiu to marry a girl from his family, so that this family bond could serve as a proof of Liu Xiu's loyalty to the rebels. So Liu Xiu married his second wife – Guo Shengtong. Soon his cousin Liu Xuan received the news that Liu Xiu had proclaimed himself Emperor Guangwu of the Han Dynasty.

China plunged into a civil war. Over the following years Emperor Guangwu took control of more and more provinces – some by force, and others by offering local rulers honors, titles, and money. His cousin "emperor" Liu Xuan was defeated, and then betrayed and killed by his own generals. The capital of the empire, Luoyang, was well-fortified and defended by an excellent garrison. Rather than undertaking the siege of the city, Emperor Guangwu suggested that the garrison surrender. But the Luoyang garrison commander was afraid that the emperor would execute him – they had fought many battles against each other. To reassure him, Emperor Guangwu sent him a note that read, "Those who pursue great goals don't remember past grievances." And the garrison opened the city gates.

Yin Lihua; Golden dragon (furniture detail) from the Han Dynasty era

Three years after Liu Xiu sent away his wife Yin Lihua, he called her back. He wanted to make her an empress, but she refused, because she had no kids, while the emperor's second wife already had two sons. So Guo Shengtong became the empress, and Yin Lihua was honored as the emperor's first love and first wife. Eventually the lucky emperor had 5 sons with each of his two wives! Emperor Guangwu loved to read and spent his free time discussing literature and Confucianism with famous scholars.

It took many years before China recovered from the destruction caused by Wang Mang's reforms and wars. But eventually prosperity returned and the population of the empire nearly quadrupled during Emperor Guangwu's reign.

Emperor Taizong
598 – 649

Throughout the centuries, Chinese historians believed that the reign of Emperor Taizong of the Tang dynasty was the "golden age" of China. Every crown prince was required to study the biography of Emperor Taizong and his policies. Every emperor was judged based on whether he came anywhere close to the glory of Emperor Taizong.

Emperor Taizong was born Li Shimin. His dad, Li Yuan, was a general in the army of the Sui dynasty that ruled for 37 years – 581 to 618. As a kid Li Shimin received the typical education of a Chinese aristocrat. It included study of Chinese literature and a lot of calligraphy. Li Shimin was so good at calligraphy that prints of his work are sold in China even today for students to copy. He was also trained in military arts and was especially good at archery. When he was a teenager, his father was appointed governor of Shansi, a mountainous region on the Western border of China, and Li Shimin's teen years were spent by the Great Wall, among the troops repelling the attacks of Turkic tribes from the steppes of Mongolia.

At that time China was ruled by Emperor Yang of the Sui dynasty – an arrogant and unpopular leader. To make his grand building projects possible, the population was taxed to the limit. He sent a giant army to fight in Korea. The Korean kingdom of Goguryeo had been a Chinese province during the Han Dynasty, but later it split away. The war was a disaster. Thousands of Chinese soldiers *deserted* (escaped from their military units) and turned to banditry and robbery. So many farm workers were *conscripted* (forced to serve in the army) that the agriculture in many areas of the country was dying. To avoid going to war farmers deliberately broke their own arms and legs.

Emperor Taizong's portrait and an example of his calligraphy work

The Sui dynasty was hated, and in some areas of the country deserters and jobless farm workers started uniting into rebel armies.

In 615, when Li Shimin was 15, Emperor Yang came to Shansi to spend the summer in a palace he had built himself in the mountains. One day, driven by curiosity, he decided to tour the steppe on the other side of the Great Wall. One of the Turkic warlords learned about it and rushed to the wall with a few thousand horsemen hoping to capture the emperor. What saved Emperor Yang was a secret warning he received from the Turkic warlord's wife, who happened to be a Chinese princess! The emperor fled to a fort built around a gate in the Great Wall, and was immediately besieged there by thousands of enemy warriors whose arrows, according to Chinese chronicles of that era, "fell like rain" on the fort. In shock, the emperor sat in a basement with his youngest son in his arms, and cried "till his eyes were swollen." His generals had no idea what to do. Men from the border towns were called to help the troops rescue the emperor. 15-year-old Li Shimin participated in the rescue mission and was praised for his courage.

Emperor Yang was saved, but he blamed the humiliation he had experienced on Li Shimin's dad, Li Yuan, who had failed to stop the raids by the Turkic tribes. Plus there was another threat. Supposedly there was an "ancient prophecy," saying that the next emperor of China would be a man with the family name Li – Li Yuan's surname! And Emperor Yang had already killed one of his officials with the surname Li fearing that his clan would claim the throne. Even though Li Yuan didn't believe in prophecies, he started thinking of running away and joining the rebels – to save himself and his family.

The Great Wall at Yanmen Pass where Emperor Yang was besieged by the Turkic warlords

Li Shimin also despised fake prophecies and "signs from heavens," but the idea of leading a rebellion and taking over the throne of China had occurred to him too. In fact, it had become his dream. More than that, secretly from his dad, Li Shimin had already discussed this with some of his father's powerful friends, and worked out a strategy for an uprising. It wasn't hard to persuade Li Yuan to go along with his kid's plan. Everyone knew the emperor was ruthless and could seize Li Yuan and his family any moment. So the rebellion began. The whole north of the country split away. Emperor Yang's troops fighting in Korea realized that they wouldn't be able to go to their homes in the north and started deserting by the thousands. To stop his soldiers from running away, Emperor Yang decided to provide his troops with new homes and new families. He ordered every soldier to find a new wife in nearby villages. This mass marriage kept his troops busy for a while. But not for long. The army revolted anyway.

In the imperial palace, Emperor Yang's generals were now conspiring to join the mutiny. They dropped all caution and were discussing this so openly that one day a lady-in-waiting came running to the empress and told her about one such conversation she had overheard. The empress was afraid to bring the bad news to Emperor Yang, so she sent the lady-in-waiting. The emperor heard the news and ordered the lady-in-waiting beheaded. He, himself, however, had only a few weeks to live. One day his military commanders marched into his throne room, surrounded him, accused him of treason, and drew swords to kill him. "Stop!" shouted Emperor Yang. "The Son of Heaven will choose how to die. Do not shed my blood, bring me poison!" But his accusers refused to waste time delivering him poison. Then the emperor gave them his scarf, and the assassins used it to strangle him right there, on his throne.

That was the end of the Sui Dynasty.

Left: Li Shimin; Right: A vase and a rider figurine with 3-color glaze, China, Tang Dynasty.

Li Yuan, Li Shimin's dad, proclaimed himself Emperor Gaozu of the new dynasty – the Tang. However the title of the crown prince, the heir to the throne, was given not to Li Shimin, but to his oldest brother Li Jiancheng. Many among Li Shimin's supporters thought this was unfair. Everyone knew it was Li Shimin's resolution and strategy that had brought them victory. But Li Shimin focused only on the struggle ahead. The country was split between 11 warlords, some of whom had also proclaimed themselves emperors. For the Tang Dynasty to survive, it was vital to unify the country once again. And it took years. Li Shimin and his brothers led Tang armies conquering China's provinces. Li Shimin was a brilliant military strategist. He defeated one of the warlords by first building a dam on the Ming River and then destroying it to cause a flood that swept away the enemy troops.

Meanwhile the split in Li Shimin's family deepened. His brothers – Li Jiancheng, his eldest brother, and Li Yuanji, his youngest brother – were intensely jealous of his victories. 17-year-old Li Yuanji was appointed governor of Shansi, but his behavior was so crazy that people were afraid to even talk about it, let alone report it to his dad. For example, as a form of a barbaric amusement, he forced his wives and their female servants to fight battles between one another and even kill one another. When he rode through city streets, he would randomly shoot arrows at passers-by "to see if they could dodge the arrows." In the evening, accompanied by a gang of friends, he broke into people's homes and spent the night there drinking alcohol and destroying their property. He wasted fortunes on expensive wines and gifts for his girlfriends. Finally, Shansi officials complained to the emperor, and the dad called the kid on the carpet. But while Li Yuanji traveled to Chang'an (present-day Xi'an), the Tang capital, Shansi was invaded by one of the competing warlords who figured out the citizens of Shansi would welcome a change of masters.

Now that both Li Shimin's brothers were in Chang'an, they united against Li Shimin. By that time their mom had died, and a few new wives were competing for their dad's attention. The two brothers sent lavish gifts to these women, and praised them to Emperor Gaozu. In exchange, the wives whispered in the emperor's ear all sorts of lies about Li Shimin. For example, they convinced him that Li Shimin was planning to murder them and their kids after the emperor's death. After Li Shimin's victory against the Turkic tribes in the north, his brothers grew so jealous and hostile, that they plotted an assassination of Li Shimin. By mere chance their plot failed and Emperor Gaozu found out about it. The brothers first considered overthrowing their dad, but were afraid that Li Shimin's army would block this action.

So they rushed to their father, confessed their crime and begged for forgiveness. The chorus of wives joined them, telling the emperor that the brothers had good reasons to be upset with Li Shimin. Predictably, the dad caved and forgave his sons. And that only encouraged the brothers to try new schemes to destroy Li Shimin.

One day the three brothers accompanied the emperor on a hunting trip. Along the way, crown prince Li Jiancheng offered Li Shimin his – supposedly – best horse. Actually, the horse was specifically chosen for its bad temper and its history of tossing riders off its back. Li Shimin attempted to ride it and, sure enough, the horse threw him off. To his brothers' disappointment Li Shimin wasn't killed. He still suspected nothing, however, and tried to mount the bad-tempered horse again. When one of the court officials warned him of the risk, Li Shimin responded, "Life and death are predestined, so what's the risk?" Well, the brothers "edited" his words just a little bit, and that evening one of the emperor's wives quoted Li Shimin to the emperor like this, "He said: I have the Mandate of Heaven and I know I will be the lord of the empire, so there's no risk." Convinced that Li Shimin wanted to seize the throne, the emperor was mad and screamed at him. But the brothers didn't stop there. A year later they organized a banquet in honor of Li Shimin's military successes and slipped poison into his wine. Li Shimin drank it and fell to the floor, vomiting blood. He lucked out and survived. His brothers poured too much poison into his cup, which caused nausea, and as Li Shimin threw up, most of the poison left his body.

In 626, having learned of his brothers' latest scheme to assassinate him, Li Shimin called together a council of friends. "If you have any doubts about your brothers' resolve to kill you, you are a fool. Take 800 of your men, storm their palace and settle the matter." That was the advice Li Shimin heard at that meeting. Li Shimin asked to cast lots and let fate decide whether he should raise his hand against his brothers. But one of his officers overturned the table with the lots. "So, if the answer is 'No,' you will just do nothing and die?" he shouted. The next morning Li Shimin and his men hid near the Xuanwu Gate of Chang'an.

The reverse side of a Tang Dynasty bronze mirror; Tang-era ceramic pillow. In ancient China, wealthy women wore intricate hairstyles. To preserve their hairstyle, they used hard pillows (wood or ceramic) placed under the neck instead of the head.

When his brothers appeared at the gate heading to the imperial court, Li Shimin shot the crown prince with an arrow through his heart. His youngest brother tried to escape, but was also killed. Li Shimin's troops took control of the capital and of the imperial palace, and forced Emperor Gaozu to appoint Li Shimin crown prince. Li Shimin ordered all the sons of his brothers – still kids – executed to prevent any claims to the throne in the future. Two months later his dad agreed to retire and Li Shimin was crowned Emperor Taizong.

Emperor Taizong's reign was a time of increasing prosperity and military success for China. The Turkic tribes on the Western borders were defeated. The empire reclaimed most of the regions it had controlled during the Han Dynasty, plus it added territories that belong to present-day Korea, Vietnam, Russia, and Central Asian countries. While things were going well in the empire, Emperor Taizong's family experienced another round of "brother trouble" – kids fighting for the throne. Taizong's oldest son, Crown Prince Li Chengqian, was fascinated with the culture and customs of the Turkic tribes – the Tatars – from the Mongolian grasslands on the other side of the Great Wall. His guards were Turkic, so Li Chengqian learned to speak their language, and started dressing in Tatar-style clothes. He loved the simplicity and the freedom of nomadic life and hated court ceremonies and the innumerable rules that prescribed the behavior of the royal family. When out hunting with his Tatar guards, he lived in a Turkic-style tent and played drums brought to him from Mongolia. His favorite entertainment was called the "Funeral of the Khan." Dressed as a Turkic **khan** (ruler), Li Chengqian lay on the ground pretending he was dead while his guards rode horses in circles around him praising his heroic deeds.

One of his younger brothers, hoping to become the crown prince, ratted on Li Chengqian to his dad, hinting that such love for foreign customs wasn't appropriate for the crown prince of China. Suspecting that the emperor would replace him with one of his brothers, Li Chengqian rebelled. He was eventually captured and exiled. But the brother who ratted on him didn't get what he wanted either. Emperor Taizong saw through his scheme. "Whoever craves power is unworthy to have it," he said, and the ratting brother was kicked out of the capital as well.

Since Emperor Taizong is one of the most colorful figures of Chinese history, there are many *historical anecdotes* – stories – about him in Chinese chronicles. Here are a few examples.

Tang-era jade dog figurine and a hair pin (gilded silver)

1

In 642 Emperor Taizong said to his chief historian, "I'd like to see what historians write about me and my reign."
"In my department we record the actions of Your Majesty no matter whether they are good or bad," responded the chief historian. "We record your words exactly, whether they are wise or disappointing... This is important, because history provides examples that teach princes and ministers, often preventing them from making mistakes."
"So you write down even things that present me in an unfavorable light?" pressed the emperor.
"How could I avoid doing so?" replied the chief historian nervously.
Then one of his assistants suddenly spoke up, "And even if you were unwilling to write that down," he said to his boss, "the rest of us, the historians who work for you, would not hesitate to record the facts."

2

Emperor Taizong's prime minister, Fang Xuanling, had a wife who screamed at her husband for any mistake or misstep he made. She was also very jealous and suspicious. One evening Fang Xuanling admitted to the emperor that he was afraid to go home to his wife. The emperor told his prime minister to marry another wife or two. And the jealous wife would be sent away to live with her parents by the order of the emperor, he suggested. When Fang Xuanling's wife was called in front of the emperor and heard his order, she screamed at the emperor too and refused to obey. "If you are going to persist in this behavior," said Emperor Taizong, "then here is a cup of poisoned wine for you – a punishment for disobeying the emperor." A cup was handed to Fang Xuanling's wife. Nobody but the emperor knew that instead of poisoned wine, the cup was filled with vinegar. To the emperor's greatest surprise, instead of begging for mercy, Fang Xuanling's wife drank the "poisoned wine" without hesitation.

"Horses" by Han Gan, the most famous painter of the Tang Dynasty (706 – 783)

The emperor was shaken by such an expression of confidence. "Now I'm afraid of her too," he whispered to Fang Xuanling and sent them both home. In China they sometimes use the expression "drinking vinegar" to describe jealousy. Now you know why.

3

Emperor Taizong's wife, Empress Zhangsun, was another strong woman at the Tang court. Emperor Taizong had enormous respect for her and occasionally asked for her advice in the matters of the state. But the empress believed it wasn't appropriate for women to give advice to men. *The Book of Documents* quotes her saying, "Hens don't announce the dawn" (roosters do). And yet she found ways to make her opinions known and taken seriously. One day Emperor Taizong came home really annoyed with his advisor and historian Wei Zheng who had criticized the emperor's ideas in front of his whole court. "I've raised him from the dust, and he treats me like this!" the emperor fumed. Zhangsun said nothing. She suddenly left the room and a few minutes later showed up wearing her best ceremonial robe and crown jewels. "What's the occasion?" asked Taizong. "They say wise and enlightened emperors find themselves advisors who are honest and straightforward in their speech. Your Majesty has just proven to me that Wei Zheng is exactly this kind of advisor, and that means you are an enlightened and wise emperor. So I put on my best clothes to honor you." The emperor never complained about Wei Zheng again.

4

One of Emperor Taizong's ministers urged the emperor to fight corruption by kicking flatterers out of his royal council, because "those who flatter you most, are the most corrupt." "Do you have a list of these flatterers?" asked Taizong. "No," responded the minister, "but if Your Majesty wishes to know who they are, just propose some foolish idea and see who jumps up to praise it." "This would certainly work," said the emperor, "but if I use deception to trick my advisors, how can I expect them to be honest with me? The emperor is the spring, and his officials are the waters that flow from it. If the spring is pure, the river is clean."

During the Tang Dynasty, paintings of beautiful women and scenes of court life were in high demand.
"Court ladies play with a doggie"
by Zhou Fang (730 – 800),

5

Soon after Emperor Taizong ascended the throne, he learned that one of his officials had accepted several bolts of expensive silk as a bribe. But instead of throwing him in jail, Taizong sent him a few chests of the best silk from the royal warehouses. When asked why the criminal had been rewarded rather than punished, Taizong responded, "If he has conscience, my gift to him will cause him more pain than any punishment. And if he is not ashamed, there's no punishment that would make him regret his actions."

The Printing Press

The earliest known printed book in the world was published in 868, in China during the Tang Dynasty. It's the Chinese-language version of the Buddhist book "The Diamond Sutra" printed with the **woodblock technique** – using blocks of wood with book pages carved into them. 150 years later Chinese engineer Bi Sheng (972 – 1051) invented the first movable type. It consisted of baked clay 'types' – tiles – each having one Chinese character (word) carved into it. The 'types' could be rearranged to make different sentences. The printing ink was made of pine resin, wax, and paper ash.

"The Diamond Sutra"; "Family" – Tang Dynasty painted pottery figures

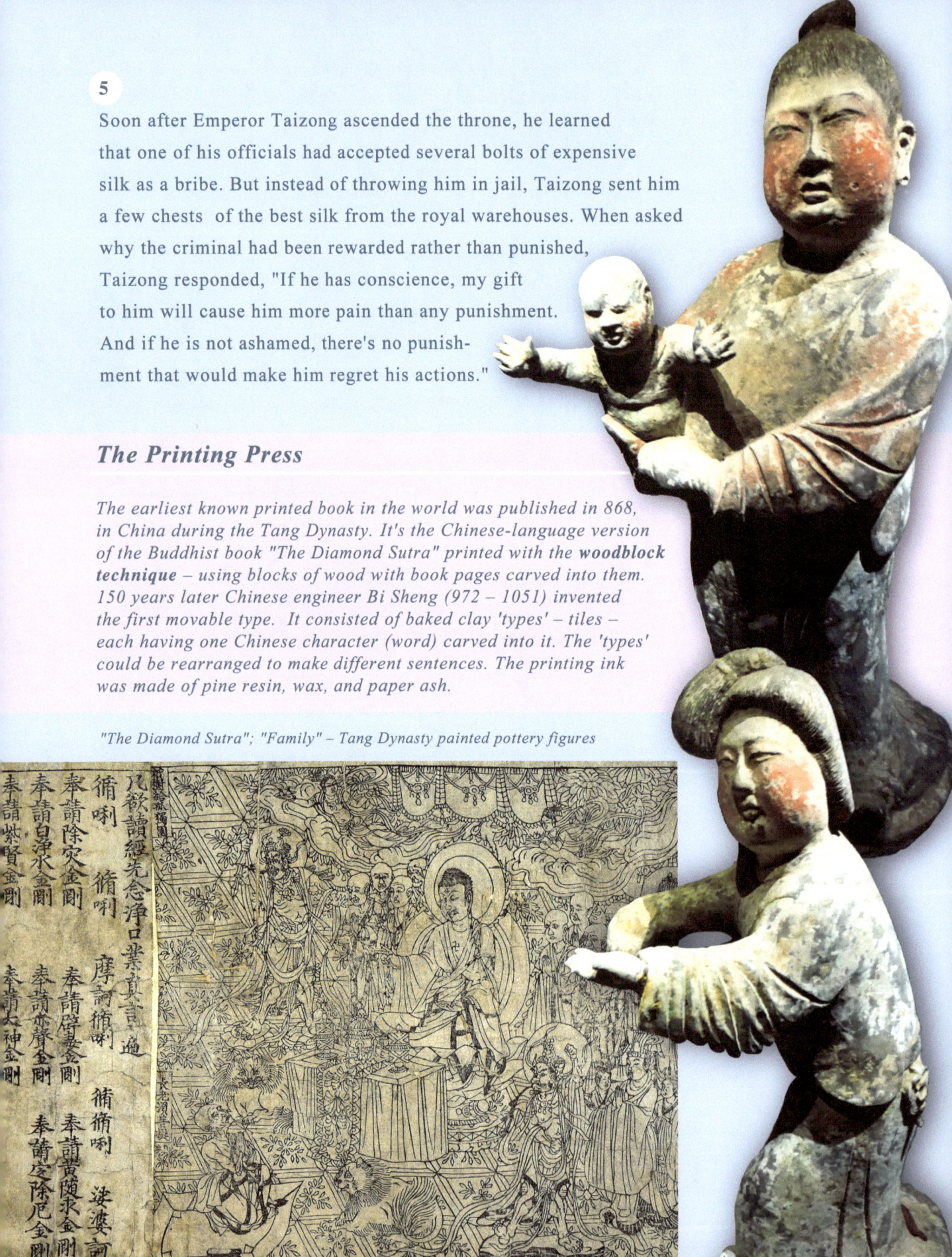

WU ZETIAN
624 – 705 BC

Wu Zetian was the only female "emperor" of China. That's right, throughout her 45-year reign she referred to herself as 'emperor,' not 'empress'! Wu Zetian started as a low-ranking wife of Emperor Taizong. Despite her low rank, however, she was so well-educated and such an excellent conversationalist, that the emperor gave her a special title – "Talented." When Emperor Taizong died, his wives who had no kids were sent to a Buddhist temple to live there as nuns. A year after Taizong's death, his 22-year-old son Emperor Gaozong came to the temple to burn incense for the anniversary of his dad's passing, and ran into Wu Zetian. When Wu Zetian saw him, she cried. Emperor Gaozong had tears in his eyes too. He remembered Wu Zetian as a stunning beauty, and now she stood in front of him dressed as a Buddhist nun, with her head shaved. Gaozong's wife, Empress Wang, noticed this and recalled rumors that her husband had been in love with Wu Zetian even before Wu became Taizong's wife. Suddenly, she suggested that the emperor bring Wu Zetian back to the royal palace. The court was shocked: Why? Well, there was a reason. Empress Wang felt that the emperor had lost interest in her and was paying too much attention to one of his other wives – Xiao. To wrestle him from her rival, the empress wanted to distract him by having him marry yet another wife – Wu Zetian. What could go wrong? Of course, her strategy backfired. Having married Wu Zetian, the emperor forgot both Wang and Xiao.

Emperor Gaozong and Wu Zetian had two sons, and in 655 Wu Zetian gave birth to a baby daughter. However the daughter died, and Wu Zetian was convinced that her daughter had been strangled by Empress Wang (who was childless and madly jealous of Wu). Perhaps, the evil Wang did this with the help of her former rival – and now an ally – Xiao, who also hated Wu Zetian... Empress Wang had no alibi. Xiao said that it was Wu herself who had killed the baby in order to falsely accuse Wang. But nobody believed that. The emperor stripped Wang of her title and imprisoned her – along with Xiao. He also made Wu Zetian empress, and made her oldest son the crown prince. A year later the emperor thought of letting Wang and Xiao go, since there was still no proof of their guilt. When Wu Zetian heard about this, she ordered Wang and Xiao to be murdered – drowned in wine barrels. Supposedly her order said, "Let these two hags get drunk to their bones!"

Emperor Gaozong

"Wu Zetian" diorama at the Henan Provincial Museum, Zhengzhou, China

When Wu Zetian's servants brought her the news that the two women were dead, they also mentioned Xiao's last words,"In the next life Wu will be born a mouse, and I will be born a cat, and I will rip her throat out!" This event cast a dark shadow on Wu Zetian's life. She was tortured by her conscience, and believed that the spirits of these two women haunted her in her dreams. She prohibited cats in the imperial palace, but its very walls reminded her of her crime. So she persuaded her husband to build her another palace. But then every street in the imperial capital, Chang'an, reminded her of Wang and Xiao. So – for this reason alone – the royal court was moved to the previous capital of China, Luoyang!

Emperor Gaozong was often sick. For weeks he didn't come "to work" as the head of his government, and Wu Zetian handled his duties for him. And even when the emperor did show up for his duties and held court in his throne hall, Wu Zetian would sit behind him concealed by a curtain and give him advice. Government officials respected her judgement, and those who criticized her were quickly replaced. 10 years after she became empress, Wu Zetian was the actual ruler of China, with her husband rarely paying any attention at all to affairs of the state. Wu had 4 sons and 2 daughters. Her oldest son, Crown Prince Li Hong, dared to criticize his mom

Alibi

Alibī ('elsewhere' in Latin) is evidence that when a crime was committed, the suspect – a person suspected of having committed the crime – was somewhere else, not on the scene of crime – and therefore not guilty of the crime.

for having seized too much power. He also made friends with the two daughters of Xiao, his half-sisters, and demanded that they be released from imprisonment and allowed to get married. When his opinions became known at the court and were whispered in every corner and behind every bush, suddenly... Prince Li Hong died! No one at the royal palace had any doubt that he had been poisoned by his own mother, Wu Zetian. Her second son, Li Xian, became crown prince. But Li Xian also had a falling-out with his mother. She accused him of treason, banished him into exile, and later ordered him to commit suicide – which he did! And then her third son, Li Zhe was made crown prince. I wonder how enthusiastic he was about that!

In 683 Emperor Gaozong died. Li Zhe was crowned Emperor Zhongzong, but – predictably – his reign lasted for only 6 weeks. His wife, Empress Wei, inspired by the example of Wu Zetian, wanted to be the power behind her husband's throne, too. But Wu Zetian was not going to share the spotlight with her son's ambitious wife. In 684 she gathered a group of royal advisors and generals, and convinced them to overthrow her son Emperor Zhongzong and replace him with her youngest son, Emperor Ruizong. By this time nobody dared to challenge the evil empress. She ignored the new emperor completely. He never even moved into the imperial quarters at the royal palace, never appeared in government councils, never received foreign ambassadors, and lived quietly, like a mouse, somewhere in the dark interior apartments of the palace. All the government officials reported to Wu Zetian, and her alone.

To boost her image as a female ruler, Wu Zetian took some steps to undermine the traditional status of the father being the head of the family. She sought to equalize gender roles in everyone's family. She declared that it was more important to be loyal to your state and your government than to your father and your family. When a father died, his family was supposed to observe a mourning period of 3 years. Wu Zetian made the mourning period for a mother the same length. When a foreign ruler would make a peace agreement with China, it was customary to send a Chinese princess to be married into his family. Imagine the shock of one foreign ruler who expected a Chinese bride for his son, but, instead of a princess, received a Chinese prince sent to him by Wu Zetian... The foreigners took it as an insult, backed out of the peace deal, and continued waging war against China. None of Wu's changes to family customs and traditions were well received. But there was something else that made her even less popular – the endless scandals around her own personal relationships.

Silver dish in the shape of a leaf, China, 7th century

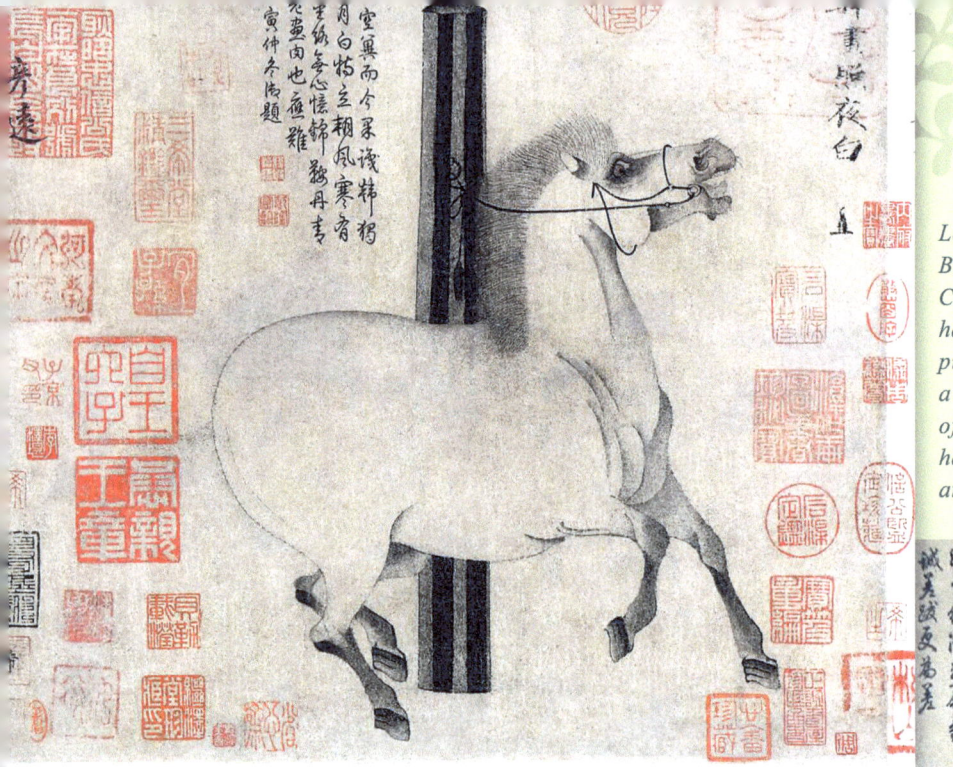

Left: "A horse" by Han Gan.
Below: "Fighting bulls" by Dai Sung.
Chinese art collectors, including emperors, have traditionally stamped the artworks they purchased with their family's seals as a sign of appreciation and confirmation of authenticity. Some famous paintings have dozens of seals to honor the artist and the family that bought his painting.

Wu Zetian raised a man by the name of Huaiyi, a women's cosmetics merchant, to some of the highest positions in the state – not because of his talents, but because he was her boyfriend. She had him ordained as a Buddhist monk so that he could come to the palace under the pretext of conducting Buddhist rituals. An arrogant and *narcissistic* (self-admiring) individual, Huaiyi expected government officials to kneel and bow in his presence and often attacked Taoist monks when he saw them in the street. Hoping to improve Huaiyi's reputation with military victories, the empress made him an army commander and sent him to fight against the Turkic nomads. But on the other side of the Great Wall, somehow Huaiyi didn't "find" the enemy army and returned home! This was the closest thing to "the dog ate my homework" in all of Chinese history! At some point Huaiyi found out that he wasn't Wu Zetian's only boyfriend. In anger he set the royal palace on fire and burned to the ground two magnificent imperial meeting halls – the Hall of Heaven and the Hall of Light. But instead of punishing him, Wu Zetian put Huaiyi in charge of palace reconstruction! Finally, Huaiyi's arrogance and craving for power made the empress uncomfortable, and she directed her guards to quietly murder him. And so we say good-bye to Huaiyi.

The rise and fall of Huaiyi was widely viewed as a disgrace brought by Wu upon all the members of the imperial family. Members of the royal Li clan rebelled but were defeated. Almost the entire Li clan died in battles or was simply executed. In 686, under pressure from her advisors, Wu Zetian offered to share power with Emperor Ruizong. But he knew his mom too well: He politely declined. Meanwhile, Wu installed special copper mailboxes on the streets of her capital, Luoyang, to collect reports of 'treason.' Anyone could report anyone else as a traitor or a spy. This innovation kept Wu Zetian's secret police busy seizing suspects and conducting investigations, usually accompanied by torture and secret executions. Anyone the empress suspected of disloyalty was falsely accused of treason and killed. Like Wang Mang 600 years before, Wu Zetian justified her claim to power by various omens (signs) and prophecies – all fake, of course. For example, in 688 her nephew 'discovered' a white stone with these words carved in it, "A wise mother will arrive and her imperial reign will flourish forever." In 690, Wu Zetian's supporters submitted to her a petition – supposedly on behalf of "the whole country" – asking her to become "emperor" herself. She "agreed," kicked her son off the throne and proclaimed a new dynasty – the Zhou.

The Imperial Examination system and Chinese Mandarins

Nationwide **civil service** *(government) exams were introduced in China during the Sui Dynasty and became standard during the Tang Dynasty. Passing these exams made you eligible to work for the imperial government. If you passed them with top scores, you were offered high positions in the imperial capital. It was a way to hire scholars and intellectuals who had talent but no wealth or connections. This system put a lot of power in the hands of people from common families, and reduced the influence of the Chinese aristocracy on the government.*

Chinese officials appointed through the imperial examination system came to be known in the West as the 'mandarins.' Of the many dialects of Chinese language, the official language adopted by the Chinese government during the Ming and Qing dynasties is called **Mandarin Chinese**. *The term 'mandarin' is not Chinese. It first appeared in the Portuguese language as a word borrowed from Malay (Malaysian language). The Malay borrowed it from Sanskrit, the ancient language of India, where "mantri" means "advisor." Chinese officials – the "mandarins" – had a special square of embroidered cloth – the* **mandarin square** *– sewn onto the front of their coats. The images on the mandarin square indicated the rank of the official. For example, a peacock was a symbol of the government officials of the 3rd rank. A crane appeared on the mandarin squares of the 1st rank. A lion was the symbol of the military officials of the 2nd rank. 3rd military rank mandarin squares featured a leopard.*

Historians believe that as the head of her government, Wu Zetian was hard-working and not without talent. She lowered taxes, helped farmers, and continued to develop the system of Imperial Examination. She even herself gave tests to men who applied to be government officials. But she couldn't resist flattery and surrounded herself with people who told her what she wanted to hear. Two of her favorites at the court were the Zhang brothers, talented young actors who flattered the old empress and amused her with songs making fun of her government officials. The Zhang brothers managed to insult everyone at the court and were much hated. As Wu Zetian was already over 80 years old, the brothers knew, once she passed away, they would be brutally murdered. In 705 they tried to steer the empress toward appointing a new crown prince – someone who supported them. Having learned about it, a bunch of top government officials decided it was time for a **palace revolution**. The conspirators forced Wu Zetian's son, former Emperor Zhongzong (who dreaded his mother and was reluctant to cross her path again) to come with them to the imperial palace accompanied by a unit of heavily-armed soldiers. At the palace they caught and beheaded the Zhang brothers and made the empress transfer power back to her son Emperor Zhongzong, restoring the Tang Dynasty.

Wu Zetian died ten months later, at age 82. According to her wish, a blank tombstone – with no inscription – was put over her grave. She meant it as an invitation to anyone to say whatever they wanted about her, including criticism – for which she had killed thousands during her lifetime.

Wu Zetian's grave stone. The inscription was added to it during the Ming Dynasty. Left: Portrait of a Chinese official with the 8th-rank "mandarin square" (quail)

KUBLAI KHAN
1215 – 1294

In the 10th century, during the last decades of the Tang dynasty, China split into kingdoms and princedoms ruled by local warlords. In 960 the Song Dynasty came to power but never fully reunified the empire. 300 years later, in 1279, the Mongol invasion toppled the Song Dynasty, and Mongolian rulers occupied the imperial throne of China as the Yuan Dynasty for almost 100 years, from 1279 until 1368.

The first Mongolian conqueror and the first *khan* (ruler) of the Mongol Empire was Genghis Khan. He unified the Mongol tribes and in 1205 attacked the kingdom of Xia in the northeast of China. The victory was easy because all Xia's troops were busy waging wars with the other Chinese kingdoms – the Jin Empire and the Song Dynasty's Empire. The Jin Empire ruler expected Genghis Khan to pay tribute to China, like the Mongols had done in the past. But when his ambassador showed up at Genghis Khan's camp demanding tribute, Genghis Khan told him some insulting jokes about the Jin emperor and asked the ambassador to write them down and tell them directly to the emperor. Next he spat at the Jin ambassador, climbed on his horse and rode away. A war broke out, of course, and soon the Jin Empire asked for peace – paying to Genghis Khan a tribute that included 3000 horses, 500 slaves, large quantities of precious silk and gold, and a Chinese princess to marry one of Genghis Khan's sons.

In 1222 Genghis Khan led his armies to deal the final blow to Xia and Jin. But during that campaign Genghis Khan fell off his horse and was badly injured. His sons urged him to go home

"A Mongol warrior" by Giuseppe Castiglione. Giuseppe Castiglione was an Italian monk and missionary who served as an artist at the Chinese imperial court in the 18th century.

In his painting, he blended Chinese and European techniques and styles.

to Mongolia and rest, but just at that time the Xia army commander sent Genghis Khan a message that was full of mockery and insults. Genghis Khan refused to leave, and died of his injury a few months later. The throne of the Mongol Empire went to Genghis Khan's middle son Ögedei. Ögedei lacked talent as a military commander and was an alcoholic, but Genghis Khan loved him for his humor, friendliness, and ability to always work out a deal or a compromise. Ögedei was very different from his two older brothers who were constantly at each other's throats. Khan Ögedei kept the Mongol Empire growing both east and west, but his reign was short. Alcoholism started seriously affecting Ögedei's health. His family and advisors made him promise to limit the amount of alcohol he consumed. But while he vowed to drink only so many cups of wine a day, he secretly ordered new cups to be made for him – twice the size of the old cups! So one day, in 1241, after a night of partying and drinking, he dropped dead. The Mongol Empire then fell into the hands of Genghis Khan's grandkids. After 30 years of the struggle for power and civil war, Genghis Khan's grandson Kublai became the Great Khan of the Mongol Empire and gave his dynasty a Chinese name, "Yuan," which means "eternal, from the beginning."

Growing up, Kublai was much influenced by his mother, Sorkhakhtani, wife of Genghis Khan's son Tolui. She was a Christian and the only person who dared to speak to Genghis Khan without fear. Genghis Khan, in his turn, never criticized her. He had a lot of respect for his grandson Kublai and advised his family, "If you are ever in doubt what to do, ask this boy Kublai." After Genghis Khan's death Kublai became the governor of Northern China. There, he made friends with a Buddhist monk named Liu Ping-chung – an artist, a poet, and a mathematician. Serving as Kublai's advisor, Liu Ping-chun educated the Mongol prince in Chinese history, literature, philosophy, and political thought. Kublai openly admired Chinese culture and governance (the manner of governing a state) and wore Chinese rather than Mongolian clothes.

Genghis Khan on a a ₮20,000 Mongolian banknote and the monument to Ogedei in Ulaanbaatar, the capital of Mongolia

That made him some enemies among the Mongols. His older brother Möngke, who ruled the Mongol Empire for 8 years after Ögedei's death, was so jealous of Kublai's growing popularity in China that he accused some of Kublai's Chinese officials of treason and had them executed.

Once Kublai won a civil war against his cousins and became the great khan of the Mongols, he led his troops against the Chinese Song Dynasty, which still existed to the south. The Song Empire army was much stronger than that of the Mongols. Some battles lasted for years. The Mongol siege of the city of Xiangyang went on for 5 years. The walls of Xiangyang were so high and massive, there was no way the Mongols could break into the city. Kublai consulted astrologers and fortune-tellers and practiced magic rituals, such as sprinkling the milk of white horses all around his military camp, but no spells could bring down the walls of Xiangyang. That's when Kublai recalled hearing of the catapults used by the armies of European crusaders. He hired two Persian engineers to build him a catapult. The new weapon worked wonders: The Xiangyang walls were breached, and the city fell, opening access to southern China.
In 1279 the Song resistance was completely crushed. Hundreds of thousands of Song Empire troops and civilians perished during a relentless Mongolian onslaught. The Song army retreated to the coast, and when the Mongols captured every port, the Chinese sailed to coastal islands and continued fighting from there. Finally, a few Chinese ships were surrounded by Kublai Khan's navy. Aboard one of them was the last Song emperor, 9-year-old Ti-ping.

Mongolian warriors

When the Mongols demanded surrender, the admiral who commanded the Chinese navy took Ti-ping in his arms, shouted out "An Emperor of the Song Dynasty would rather die than live as a prisoner!" and jumped in the ocean, drowning himself and Ti-ping. 800 generals and members of the Song royal family followed the admiral's example and drowned themselves in the sea to avoid the humiliation of captivity.

On that day, for the first time in its history, China fell under foreign rule. And there was yet another important outcome of Kublai's conquest: For the first time since the fall of the Tang Dynasty in the 10th century, China was again reunited. Kublai Khan realized the historical significance of China's reunification. He had a Chinese-style coronation, proclaiming himself the 'Son of Heaven' and heir to the nineteen imperial Chinese dynasties before him. He had already won respect in Northern China with his commitment to preserve Chinese civilization, embrace Chinese culture and promote Buddhism and Taoism. Now, to gain support across the whole empire, Kublai went even further. He hired Chinese scholars as advisors, let many of the Song Dynasty officials continue working in the government, and kept Confucianism as the state religion. He also published a decree stating that although the Mongols were better warriors than the Chinese, there was something they needed to learn from the Chinese – the skills of running government and governing the country. With all that, Kublai Khan knew, of course, that the Chinese viewed the Mongols as uncultured barbarians. He didn't trust them one bit, and filled top government positions with foreigners – not only Mongols, but even Europeans. For instance, travellers from Venice – Marco Polo, his dad and his uncle – were all hired as governors and diplomats by Kublai Khan even though they had zero experience and didn't know how to run a government.

In the West, Kublai Khan is best remembered through the writings of Marco Polo and from the poem *Kubla Khan* by the 19th-century English poet Samuel Taylor Coleridge who echoed Marco Polo's reports:

In Xanadu did Kubla Khan
A stately pleasure-dome decree:
Where Alph, the sacred river, ran
Through caverns measureless to man
Down to a sunless sea.

So twice five miles of fertile ground
With walls and towers were girdled round;
And there were gardens bright with sinuous rills,
Where blossomed many an incense-bearing tree;
And here were forests ancient as the hills,
Enfolding sunny spots of greenery...

The 'stately pleasure dome' in Coleridge's poem was a large Mongol tent in the middle of a hunting park laid out in Shangdu (Xanadu) – the summer-time capital of Kublai Khan's court.

Kublai's "chief wife," Chabi, was a remarkable woman. She gave her husband advice in political and government matters, helped the families of defeated warlords and generals to escape prison and execution, and was a fashion designer! Chabi designed a Mongol-style hat with a wide brim and a sleeveless tunic for Mongol foot soldiers to wear under the hot sun of Southern China. Chabi died in 1281, and Kublai Khan, who was 66, never recovered from this loss. When 4 years later his oldest son and heir also died, Kublai sank into deep depression and withdrew from day-to-day government work. The only time anyone ever saw him was when he came out to hunt in one of his hunting parks. He gained so much weight that he wasn't able to use a bow, so he hunted with a trained cheetah that rode with him on his horse, or with a trained tiger, or with a hawk.

Kublai Khan's reign was marked by many historically-important events and achievements. He made Beijing the capital of China. During his era the Chinese started actively using paper money. The Mongols defeated the Koreans and attempted to conquer Japan – twice, but both times failed. The Yuan era was rich in cultural achievements: Chinese visual arts, literature and theater flourished. But the Yuan Dynasty lasted for only 97 years. It lost control over Mongolia, and in China decades of discrimination against the native Han Chinese resulted in rebellions and a war of liberation. Eventually the last Yuan emperor was chased out of China back to the grasslands beyond the Great Wall.

Kublai's wife Chabi, wearing the "Gugu hat" – the tall headdress of noble Mongolian women. "Gugu" was a Mongolian word for "hat."

Oh no! "Chinese buttons" are not Chinese!

Believe it or not, the use of buttons in clothing was introduced to China by the Mongols! Before the Yuan Dynasty, the Chinese used only belts and ties to keep their robes closed. The knot-and-loop button, which is often called the "Chinese button," came to China from Mongolia.

Marco Polo

In 1260, the two Polo brothers, merchants from Venice, reached China and visited the court of Kublai Khan. On the way back they delivered a message from Kublai to the Pope in Rome. 15 years later the brothers returned to China. This time they were accompanied by 17-year old Marco Polo who later described his travels in his famous book *The Travel Notes of Marco Polo*. Kublai liked Marco Polo and invited him to stay at his court. Marco lived in China, and traveled across the Yuan Empire for 17 years. He was even appointed the governor of Yangzhou, a city in East China. The Polos left China to return to Venice in 1292, arriving home 3 years later.

In his book, Marco Polo described Kublai Khan's palaces, his hunting expeditions, and the customs of his court. He also noticed that the Mongols relied on a massive police force to prevent resistance to their rule. "Every inn-keeper has to register his guests' names and surnames, as well as the day and month of their arrival and departure," wrote Marco Polo. "This way the emperor has the means of knowing, whenever it pleases him, who comes and goes throughout his empire. Also after the Great Khan occupied the city [Beijing] he ordered that each of the city's 12,000 bridges (!!) should be guarded by ten men in case anyone plotted treason or uprising against him..."

Here is Marco Polo's report on coal (virtually unknown in Medieval Europe): "All over the country of Cathay (China) there is a kind of black stone which they dig out and burn like firewood. If you put these stones in the fire in the evening, you will find them still burning in the morning, and they make such fine fuel that no other is used throughout the country. It is true that they have plenty of wood also, but they do not burn it, because those stones burn better and cost less. Moreover, with the vast number of people and the number of baths they take – at least three times a week, and in winter, if possible, every day – wood would not suffice for the purpose."

Among Polo's reports on Mongol customs, there is one really scary: "Let me tell you a strange thing too. When they carry the body of their king to be buried, they put to the sword (kill) anyone whom they happen to see on the road. Because they believe that anyone they kill will go to serve their king in the other world. They do the same with horses. When the king dies, they kill all his best horses, in order that he may have the use of them in the other world, as they believe. And I tell you as a certain truth, that when Möngke Khan [Kubilai's brother] died, more than 20,000 persons, who chanced to meet the body on its way, were killed in the manner I have told you."

THE HONGWU EMPEROR
1328 – 1398

Following a century under Mongol military occupation, China was a mess. The country's social order had been wrecked. China's native ruling class – its landowners – had been mostly killed off by the Mongols of the Yuan Dynasty. So when the anti-Yuan uprising began, its leaders were people from the lowest social classes. The founder of the Ming Dynasty, Zhu Yuanzhang, was born in a poor peasant family.

When he was 15, Zhu Yuanzhang's parents died in a plague epidemic, and his older brothers starved to death. "The people in my village lacked food. They ate grass and bark," reads the text of the *Imperial Tomb Tablet of the Great Ming*, Zhu Yuanzhang's own account of his life carved in stone after he became the emperor of China. A homeless orphan suffering from hunger and abuse, Zhu Yuanzhang found shelter at a Buddhist temple. Buddhist monks taught him to read and write, but they couldn't afford to feed him, so he left, traveling on foot around China begging for food. "Turning to my relatives would have been shameful, so I could only raise my face to boundless Heaven," recalls Zhu in the *Tomb Tablet* text. "With no one to rely on, my shadow became my companion."

The Ming Dynasty

The Ming Dynasty (1368 – 1644) was one of the most prosperous eras in Chinese history. It lasted for 276 years. One of its most remarkable features was the use of the Imperial Examination to create a new ruling class. Any man could take an Imperial Examination test to see if he qualified to work in the government. Government officials – from a lowly clerk to the prime minister himself – were not allowed to stay in the capital after they retired. Everyone had to go home to their native town. Government salaries were small. Many top officials had to run farms and other businesses to provide for their families. Criticizing the emperor was encouraged! Officials who dared to speak the truth to the emperor's face were honored for their courage and integrity. To prevent powerful clans from interfering with the emperor's policies, members of the royal family and aristocracy were not allowed to be involved in politics. For the same reason, empresses were chosen from lower-class families.

Some social policies of the Ming-era imperial government were way ahead of their time. To promote literacy and education, bookseller businesses were free of tax. Wealthy families paid for free medical care, and for funerals for the poor across China. If they failed to pay these costs, their property was seized by the government. Homeless shelters were established in every town. In families where parents were over 70, one of their sons was allowed to stop paying taxes so he had extra money to care for his elderly parents. To people over 80, whose kids couldn't provide for them, the government gave free meat and wine.

Walking from village to village, Zhu saw the utter despair of common people whose lives were destroyed by enormous taxes, civil war, poverty, hunger, and catastrophic floods of the Yellow River. Many left their homes and joined bands of rebels seeking to overthrow the Yuan Dynasty. Zhu returned to his Buddhist monastery, but soon it was burned down by the Mongols who suspected the Buddhists of spreading anti-Yuan ideas. Around that time Zhu, now 25, ran into a childhood friend who invited him to join one of the rebel groups. Zhu Yuanzhang recalled his thoughts about joining the rebellion, "I could either have my hands bound like a criminal, or raise my arms in resistance and end up killed." He became first a soldier and then a unit commander – thanks to his ability to read and write.

Zhu Yuanzhang's unit was part of an army led by rebel commander General Guo. Guo appreciated Zhu's intelligence and friendly personality. He noticed that Zhu liked Ma Xiuying, Guo's adopted daughter, and suggested that Zhu and Ma get married. If someone told 20-year-old Ma on her wedding day that 15 years later she would be the empress of China, sitting on a throne and dripping with pearls and emeralds, she would have fallen off her chair laughing. General Guo's friendship with Zhu made some rebel leaders jealous. They accused Zhu of being a Yuan spy. Zhu Yuanzhang was thrown in jail where they didn't give him food for days in a row. His wife Ma Xiuying, smuggled rice cakes into his prison cell. She wanted Zhu to eat the cakes while they were still hot, so her chest was covered with burns because she hid them under her clothes.

Empress Ma

In 1353, when Zhu Yuanzhang was finally released, he no longer wanted to fight under the command of General Guo or other rebel leaders. He returned to his hometown and recruited 24 men – his childhood friends and friends of friends – to fight against the Mongols. He was their commander. Since Zhu was already known for his courage and decisiveness, more and more volunteers joined him, and soon he had 700 men. His 24 friends were now unit commanders. These were the future generals of the Ming Dynasty. The rebels lived in desperate poverty, eating whatever they could collect in the woods or find in the ruins of abandoned barns and farmhouses. Ma rarely had a meal – she saved most of the food she could find for her husband.

Unlike most rebel armies, Zhu Yuanzhang's troops were not allowed to force farmers to supply them with food. "We must not take a single thing from them," he said. "If we have their support, there will be no battle we cannot win." He had his soldiers rotate between doing farm work and military duty. Ma Xiuying made shoes and sewed clothes for rebel troops. One time when Zhu Yuanzhang was wounded, she saved his life by carrying him to safety on her back. Zhu Yuanzhang and Ma had 5 sons and 2 daughters. They also adopted some orphaned kids.

Seven years after he joined the revolt against the Mongols, Zhu Yuanzhang controlled a large territory with millions of inhabitants. His army numbered hundreds of thousands of well-trained warriors. China was now divided between a few rebel warlords, and a clash between them was inevitable. After 8 more years of war, the rebel states in the south of China were defeated, and in 1368, 40-year-old Zhu Yuanzhang proclaimed himself emperor. He gave his dynasty the name "Ming" – "Radiance." He also gave a special name to his reign – Hongwu – "Great Military Success," and is called the Hongwu Emperor.

A few months later Zhu Yuanzhang's troops marched toward the capital of the Yuan Empire, Beijing. The Mongol army engaged them in a battle outside the city. Meanwhile, in the imperial palace, the last emperor of the Yuan Dynasty, Toghon Temür, worked on an astrological chart, trying to predict the outcome of the battle by the stars. The verdict of the stars was clear to him: His empire was in its last days. So he packed, sneaked out of the city, and escaped to the other side of the Great Wall. The Yuan army followed their emperor. In the following years Zhu Yuanzhang unified China, and even attempted to conquer Mongolia, but failed.

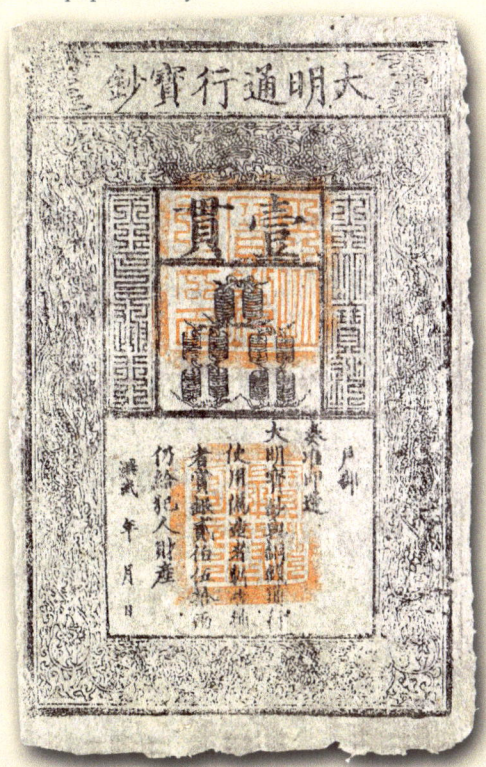

A Ming Dynasty banknote – paper money

Zhu Yuanzhang and Empress Ma never forgot the hardships of their youth. Even as an empress, Ma kept cooking her own meals and sewing her clothes. She wore her clothes until they had holes. Zhu Yuanzhang also rejected luxury and instructed his family and government officials to live modestly.
He ordered his sons to replace flower gardens in their palaces with vegetable gardens growing food for their kitchens. He banned exotic pets, like tigers, and encouraged his court to raise cows instead. He prohibited using rice to make wine. Rice was only for food.

If landowners failed to pay taxes on their land, their land was taken away from them and redistributed among the poor. And since most landowners cheated on taxes, thousands of wealthy families lost their land. Zhu Yuanzhang also seized the land of many Buddhist monasteries and gave it to the peasants. Over 3000 monasteries were shut down and their inhabitants sent to work on the farms.

Zhu Yuanzhang also sought to limit the wealth of the merchant class. He banned all trade by sea, closed all ports and blocked harbors with rocks. Building ships with more than one mast was prohibited. Nobody was allowed to leave China, and foreigners were not allowed in – the sea coast was heavily guarded. To limit the power of the military, the top positions in the army were given to Zhu Yuanzhang's sons. The day they turned 20, they were sent as military commanders to Chinese provinces, and not allowed – under punishment of death – to ever come back to the capital of the empire, Nanjing. This was to prevent rivalry between the princes.

Roof Charms

The roofs of the imperial palaces and government buildings in China were usually decorated with ceramic figures of mythological creatures. Farthest from the edge was always the imperial dragon. Closest to the edge was a man riding a Phoenix – a symbol of officials serving the emperor. Other creatures included a bull protecting the structure from evil spirits, a lion, and a good luck seahorse. The maximum number of figures was nine – on the roofs of the imperial palaces.

Zhu Yuanzhang was ruthless with his own government officials, always suspecting them of corruption, laziness, and wasting his time. In 1375 a secretary at the Ministry of Justice submitted to Zhu a long report that started with the criticism of the imperial justice system and ended with ideas how to reform it. The problem was, the emperor had no patience to listen to the end of that 17,000-character-long report. (We are talking Chinese characters, most of which are words!) Somewhere around the 16,370th character the emperor yawned and ordered the author of the report flogged (beaten) as a punishment for criticising the justice system without proposing any improvements. The next day the emperor finished listening to the report and was amazed at the great ideas and proposals contained in its last 500 characters. He praised the Ministry of Justice secretary, admitted punishing him had been a mistake, and advised him to write shorter reports.

When Empress Ma was 50, she fell very ill. Zhu ordered his court officials to arrange for sacrifice ceremonies and prayers for her recovery. But the empress asked him to cancel everything. "Life and death are the law of nature," she said, "All these ceremonies are a waste of money." When the empress died, it was a blow to Zhu Yuanzhang. He mourned her in deep sadness. Then, in 1391, his oldest son, the crown prince, suddenly died. This was not only the emperor's personal loss, but an event that could destroy the new empire. Zhu needed to choose a new heir to the throne, but even though he trusted his sons, he was afraid that after he passed away they would start a fight for the throne. In the end he appointed one of his grandsons the new crown prince. He knew that didn't really solve the problem. His kids could still tear the country apart fighting for the crown. Zhu was also suspicious of his generals, many of whom had their daughters married to his sons. He thought they were likely to conspire against the new crown prince. So he started a purge – a mass slaughter of his own generals – his old friends. He didn't spare their clan members and supporters. Tens of thousands – some historians say, 100 thousand were charged with treason and executed.

Even though this nearly destroyed Zhu Yuanzhang's image as a wise and caring ruler, his concerns turned out to be well-grounded. Years later, after his death, one of his sons, Zhu Di, started a civil war against the new emperor, Zhu Yuanzhang's grandson. After 3 years of fighting Zhu Di seized the capital of the empire Nanjing and crowned himself the Yongle Emperor. His nephew, Zhu Yuanzhang's grandson, perished in the fire that accompanied the storming of the imperial palace.

THE FORBIDDEN CITY

When Zhu Di became the Yongle Emperor, he moved the capital from Nanjing back to Beijing, and in 1406 he started construction of the imperial palace in the center of the city. Only the emperor, his family, and their servants were allowed in the palace, so it became known as the Forbidden City. The Forbidden City was the residence of the Ming and Qing dynasties emperors from 1420 to 1924. It is surrounded by 45 walls and a moat. There is also a small artificial river with 5 bridges – the Inner Golden Water River – crossing its grounds. There are 980 buildings in the Forbidden City. Among them are:

- The Hall of Supreme Harmony – the imperial throne hall featuring the Dragon Throne
- The Palace of Heavenly Purity – the palace of the emperor and empress
- The Hall of Preserving Harmony – the royal reception and banquet hall

The Forbidden City: a corner tower and the moat; the Hall of Supreme Harmony

Tang Yin

1470 – 1524

Tang Yin was a painter and poet of the Ming Dynasty era – one of the biggest names in the history of Chinese art. Tang Yin's father ran a small restaurant in the city of Suzhou, but he dreamed of a government career for his talented son. Tang Yin amazed his teachers with his abilities as a writer and calligrapher, and he studied hard preparing for the Imperial Examination. When he was 15, his hard work paid off: He was awarded first place in the Imperial Examination in his town. Artists, writers, scholars, as well as the wealthy and powerful families of Suzhou invited him to their homes. His life was carefree, he was a local celebrity. Tang Yin got married and spent a lot of time painting and writing poetry. But around the time he turned 24 a tragedy struck his family. His parents, wife and son died in an epidemic. As Tang Yin mourned his family, his only distraction was preparing for the second round of the Imperial Examination. This time he was to compete with scholars not only from his town, but from the whole province of Nanjing where Suzhou was located.

Four years later Tang Yin took the second-round examination and won first place. He got re-married and started preparing for the national examination held in Beijing. If he passed it with a good score, he would qualify for a prestigious government position in the capital. He traveled to Beijing together with another scholar, Xu Jing, a young man from a wealthy family. The two became friends. In Beijing Tang Yin did so well in the Imperial Examination, that his name was on the list of the three highest score winners of that year. But then another disaster struck. He was accused of bribing a servant of one of the scholars who conducted the exam.

"Wild Water" – a poem and painting by Tang Yin

Supposedly the servant was paid to steal the examination questions and give them to Tang Yin and Xu Jing so they could prepare their answers in advance! Instead of being awarded honors and government jobs, the two friends were jailed. The charges against them were ungrounded. Apparently, Tang Yin had felt so well-prepared that he had bragged to other exam participants before the test that he would get the top score. The exam was extremely difficult that year, and, by sheer coincidence, the only two participants who gave all the correct answers were Tang Yin and his friend Xu. So they were reported as cheaters.

The two friends were forbidden to ever participate in the Imperial Examination again. Tang Yin's dreams and his reputation were destroyed. The only job he could find in Beijing was the position of a clerk at some low-level government office. Depressed and disheartened, he refused to take it and went home. But in Suzhou his "friends" and wealthy patrons turned away from him. Nobody wanted to be seen around "the cheater." His second wife left him (taking all his money with her). Tang Yin turned to alcohol and sank into poverty. All his friends passed the Imperial Examination and had fancy jobs in Beijing and Nanjing. There was nobody to help him. He lived in an old house that was falling apart. His circle of friends consisted of other alcoholics and outcasts. The only light in this darkness was art. To make his living Tang Yin sold his paintings.

10 years after the disaster in Beijing, a king of one of the Chinese states that paid tribute to the Ming Empire invited Tang Yin to work in his government. Tang Yin was excited, but when he started on his job, he discovered that the king was secretly preparing a rebellion against the Ming Dynasty. The soldiers were trained. The weapons were stockpiled. Tang Yin thought of going home, but now that he knew the king's secret, he realized he would be killed if he tried to escape. So he decided to pretend that he had gone insane. He ran naked in the streets like a lunatic telling passers-by that he was the king's guest of honor. He ate garbage and embarrassed himself in every imaginable way.

"Court Ladies" by Tang Yin

The king was puzzled, but he fell for the trick believing that Tang Yin had indeed gone crazy. So Tang Yin was sent back to Suzhou – where he died of alcoholism.

About a 100 years later Chinese novelist and poet Feng Menglong wrote a play *Three Words* based on a story – perhaps a legend – from Tang Yin's life. The story went like this: A Beijing government official was passing through Suzhou on his boat. Tang Yin saw the boat in the port and spotted a beautiful girl on deck. He fell in love with her at first glance, but she turned out to be a slave in the official's family, and there was no way to get in touch with her. Tang Yin pretended to be a slave and got himself sold to the same official! After many adventures he eventually gained freedom for his beloved and himself, and brought her home. The play was a huge success, and in the 20th century its plot was adapted for a number of movies and TV shows in China.

Tang Yin's poems:

Ten thousand miles of mountains

Back from the drama of the empire's capital,
In rags I return to my old thatched hut,
Where there's barely room to stand...
Yet ten thousand miles of mountains and rivers
Flow from under my brush, and come to life...

Deep in the mountains

Wild water, an abandoned pavilion,
the feeling of isolation...
Few visitors come here, deep in the mountains.
A flock of birds flies home to their nests,
and in the misty dusk clouds grow darker.
A solitary traveler faces the west wind
full of autumn leaves.

Who ruled China during the lifetime of Tang Yin? The Hongzhi Emperor and the Zhengde Emperor... wait till you read about them!

The Emperor who invented the toothbrush

Zhu Youcheng, the Hongzhi Emperor who was the 9th emperor of the Ming Dynasty, reigned from 1487 to 1505. He was one of the best rulers in Chinese history, as well as a talented musician, poet, and painter. His reign brought prosperity to China. His time was also peaceful – the emperor did not start a single war! He is remarkable for being the only emperor in the history of China who had only one wife. No multiple wives and girlfriends! Another astounding fact about the Hongzhi Emperor is that he invented the toothbrush with bristles. When you brush your teeth, think – this toothbrush was invented in 1498 in Beijing! Zhu Youcheng's toothbrush was a bamboo stick with bristles from the neck of a pig attached to it. When this invention became known in Europe, Europeans started manufacturing toothbrushes using horse hair. In 1780 English businessman William Addis created the version of a toothbrush we use today: The handle was made from cow bone, and the bristles were again pig hair – just like the original invention thought-up by the Hongzhi Emperor.

The Emperor who never grew up

Sadly, the Hongzhi Emperor died of a disease when he was only 35 years old. In 1505 one of his two sons, Zhu Houzhao became the Zhengde Emperor – the 11th emperor of the Ming dynasty. He was only 13 and completely uninterested in being a ruler. The youngest of his ministers and advisors was 56. Zhu Houzhao yawned listening to government reports and dreamed of escaping from his spectacular Forbidden City palace. What he really liked was playing music and enjoying wrestling, acrobatics, magic shows, and fireworks. He also liked role playing – pretend-play.

And since he was the emperor, everyone at his court had to play with him. He made his government officials dress up as merchants and he set up fake "shops." The emperor pretended he was a common man in the street visiting their shops. And his ministers had to do their best selling their "goods" to him. Any official who refused to participate in these pretend-play activities was fired.

Zhu Houzhao built himself a 200-room palace called the Leopard Quarter – next to the imperial zoo. The emperor and his friends spent days there partying and pretending they were on a hunt in the jungle, while, actually, hunting zoo animals. When the emperor was 25, his advisors – hoping to get rid of him – suggested that he lead his troops to fight the Mongols in Northwest China rather than kill caged animals in the zoo. Riding at the head of his army, Zhu Houzhao left Beijing and 5 days later arrived at the Great Wall gate in the Juyong Pass. However, since the government wasn't used to any grownup behavior from him, the official in charge of the gate refused to open it to the emperor and his army! "Bring me a letter signed by both your mom and your wife. Then I'll open the gate," he said. The emperor turned around and returned to Beijing!

When, eventually, the emperor made it to the Northwest, he loved being away from Beijing so much, he decided to stay there. He also came up with a new role-playing idea. He pretended he was one of his own generals – an imaginary character named General Zhu Shou. He ordered his military commanders to take this or that message to General Zhu Shou. Then he dressed as a general and listened to his own orders as General Zhu Shou. Occasionally he acted surprised and even shocked at the messages he heard. But the most remarkable part of that adventure was that Zhu Houzhao actually led his troops into battle against the Mongols and won! It was the only Chinese victory over the Mongols in the 16th century. The emperor's end, however, was pathetic. He got drunk on a fishing trip, fell off the boat into icy water, caught a cold, and died at 29.

Imperial Examination: cheaters & cheat sheets

During the Imperial Examination, men hoping for government jobs worked on their answer sheets while sitting in tiny cubicles called "cells." They lived in their cells for several days. Each man's answer sheet was copied by a scribe so that his handwriting wasn't recognized – to prevent the professors from giving higher grades to their favorite students. Even though cheating was severely punished, in some cells they found cheat sheets with text and numbers written by the cheaters as small as 1/8th the size of a rice kernel!

Beijing Imperial Examination 'cells' →

Lin Zexu
1785 – 1850

In the 16th century the Ming Dynasty opened China to foreign trade in order to export silk, porcelain, and tea to Europe. European ships were again allowed to sail into Chinese ports. In the 17th-18th centuries Chinese imports were crazily popular in Europe.

Chinoiserie

The French word 'Chinoiserie' (she-noo-ahz-ree) came to describe Chinese style and themes in fashion, interior design, and everyday items. European artists, craftsmen and manufacturers imitated Chinese goods. **Dutch pottery and tiles** echoed blue-and-white Ming-era porcelain. The famous German **Meissen china** factory produced vases, dishes and teapots with Chinese-style dragons, blooming trees, and scenes of the Chinese royal court, and also of Chinese life in the countryside. English furniture maker Thomas **Chippendale** produced tea tables and china cabinets finished in black lacquer and painted with Chinese-style landscapes. Every palace had hand-painted "birds and flowers" imitations of Chinese wallpaper and replicas of Chinese pavilions and pagodas (tiered towers) in its gardens. In Europe of the 17th and 18th centuries, having imported Chinese goods at home and drinking Chinese tea signaled that you were worldly, educated, and wealthy.

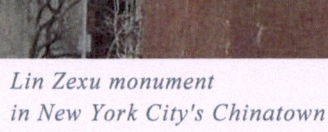

Lin Zexu monument in New York City's Chinatown

Chinese black lacquered hall stand (mid 19th century) made for export to Europe, and blue-and-white Ming-era vase; European imitations: English Wedgwood plate and a Dutch Delft hand-painted tile

German Meissen china – a teapot with a scene of "life in China" (18th century); Below: a Chinese silk wall hanging and British tea clipper "Spirit of the Age"

Porcelain

The word **porcelain** comes from 'porcellana' – a glossy shiny **cowrie shell.** That was the word used by Marco Polo, from whom Europeans first heard about Chinese porcelain. In English we also call it 'china' – because porcelain was invented in China! It was already in wide use in China during the Han Dynasty (25 – 220). By the time of the Tang Dynasty (618 – 907) Chinese artisans learned to make porcelain white and translucent – the qualities that so amazed the Europeans. In the 14th century, during the Ming era (1368 – 1644), Europeans started purchasing huge quantities of Chinese porcelain goods, as well as copying them in Europe. Porcelain was called 'white gold.' But what was it, really? In China, porcelain was made of fired **kaolin clay** and ground minerals, like alabaster. In England, in 1748, craftsmen trying to imitate Chinese porcelain invented **bone china** – porcelain made from a mix of bone ash (burnt animal bones) and kaolin. This invention contributed to the "china craze," since bone china can be very translucent and at the same time durable.

While 'chinoiserie' imitations sold well, the Europeans craved authentic Chinese imports. So streams of merchant ships delivered Chinese silks, wallpapers, porcelain, and furniture to European ports. And then there was tea.

Tea

The English word "tea" comes from "te," the word for tea in the Chinese dialect of Fujian, a province located in South China where the British purchased tea. The northern Chinese pronounced this word as "cha," so, for example, in Russian, tea is called "chai" because the Russians purchased tea in the north of China. The Chinese started making a tea drink by boiling tea leaves during the Han Dynasty. During the Tang Dynasty tea drinking spread to Korea and Japan. In the 17th century Dutch traders started bringing tea to Europe. But in Europe, tea did not become popular right away. In 1636 a Mongolian khan offered to send 250 pounds of Chinese tea as a gift to the Russian Tsar Michael I. The Russian ambassador politely refused the gift: He thought sending a load of dry leaves to the tsar was meant as an insult. But the Mongols insisted, and by the end of the 17th century Russians started buying vast quantities of tea in exchange for furs and dominated the overland tea trade. Meanwhile, on the seas, the "tea clippers" – sailing ships built for speed – carried tea from China to Europe and the Americas.

The Qing Dynasty

In the 19th century China was ruled by its last imperial dynasty – the Qing (pronounced 'ching'). The Qing emperors came from Manchuria (present-day northeast China and part of Russia) and belonged to the Manchu people (a non-Chinese minority in present-day China). They seized the Ming capital Beijing in 1644 and ruled China until 1912 when, following a revolution, the last Qing emperor was overthrown.

The Opium Wars

The Chinese government prohibited the export of tea plants and seeds to the West. Europeans were unable to grow tea in regions under their control until the 19th century. So they purchased tea from China, always trying to pay for it with European goods. But European goods were not in demand in China, so in 1685 the Chinese announced that imports from China must be paid for only in silver. To earn silver, British merchants started growing opium in India, and then bringing it to China, where they would sell it...only for silver! By the 19th century, opium addiction in China became a serious nation-wide problem, but when the Chinese government banned opium, Britain waged wars against China, pretending they were fighting to protect "free trade." The two Opium Wars (1839 – 1842, 1856-1860) were a tragic turn in the history of China. The European powers crushed the Qing Empire's army and carved China into "spheres of influence." The unfair peace treaties imposed on the Chinese allowed Europeans to govern chunks of China's territory as their own colonies.

The first "crack" in the relations between China and Britain occurred at the end of the 18th century, when British ambassador Macartney refused to *kowtow* to the Qing emperor. In Mandarin Chinese "kow" means "knock, bump," and "tow" means "head." To "kowtow" to the emperor you had to bow, then kneel, and then touch the floor with your forehead 9 times.

The Chusan Conference of 1840 – negotiations between the Chinese and the British during the First Opium War.

Opium is made from the pods of poppy plants. It's an extremely addictive drug that debilitates, disables, and kills its users.

This ritual was accepted by all nations doing business with China. But Macartney demanded that, if he kowtowed to the emperor, the imperial officials would have to kowtow to the portrait of King George III which he had brought with him. A scandal erupted. Even a shipload of gifts Macartney had brought for the emperor couldn't save his mission. The gifts included telescopes, globes, clocks, musical instruments, horse carriages, and even a hot-air balloon with a balloonist! The only item that the Chinese found interesting was a box of matches. After Macartney left, the emperor wrote the following letter to the king of England: "Our customs are different from yours, and even if your ambassador were competent enough to learn about them, they wouldn't be respected in your barbaric land. Exotic and expensive objects do not interest me. As your ambassador can see for himself, we have all the same stuff here. These items are of no value to us and we have no interest in goods manufactured in your country."

A few decades later, in the 19th century, English cotton factories started using steam engines to manufacture textiles. English fabrics were in high demand in India. To pay for them, the Indians sold more and more opium to the British. The British brought it to China, where the ports were soon jammed with opium traffic. To request more ports opened for trade, a new ambassador was sent to China in 1816, but his mission also failed – because he, too, would not kowtow! Chinese officials proposed that he kowtow to the emperor's empty throne in the empty throne hall in the middle of the night... They woke up ambassador Amherst and brought him all the way to kneeling

Chinese opium addicts smoking opium pipes in an 'opium den' (19th-century photos)

in front of the emperor's empty throne, but when it came to hitting the floor with his forehead, Amherst refused. One of the Chinese officials pushed him — hoping maybe if he fell down, his head would touch the floor — but Amherst's assistant caught him! As a result, Amherst was not allowed to see the Emperor and left with nothing.

The opium addiction had a disastrous impact on the Chinese economy. It disrupted the work of the factories, farms, ports, and government. The Chinese authorities estimated that 4 to 12 million people — mostly men between ages of 20 and 55 — became drug addicts, but European doctors working in China suspected the number was actually 3 times higher. Whenever the government tried to interfere with the opium trade, riots followed. Still, in 1837, Chinese authorities burned the boats of drug dealers in Canton and arrested many opium merchants. They had widespread public support. The owner of a popular **opium den** (a shop where people came to purchase and smoke opium) was sentenced to death. But moments before his execution 80 British sailors attacked the executioners and the crowd that gathered to watch him die. In response 6000 Chinese gathered outside the American warehouses in the port throwing stones at the foreigners.

Lin Zexu (pronounced 'ze-shu') was a Qing government official who is considered a national hero in China for his role in fighting against the British opium trade. Lin had a nickname — "Blue Sky," because his reputation was as perfect as the cloudless sky. He was a son of a poor teacher in Fujian where most of the opium arrived. Growing up, he saw families and whole neighborhoods devastated by drug use. In 1839, when the Qing Dynasty finally banned opium, Lin Zexu was tasked with enforcing the ban. He arrived in Guangzhou, a Chinese port on the Pearl River flowing into the South China Sea, and ordered local opium traders to hand their opium over to the Chinese authorities. Failure to obey the order was punishable by death. Lin fired 54 local government officials suspected of accepting bribes from the British. He ordered schoolteachers to ban opium smoking in schools. He threatened drug addicts with execution if they didn't quit opium within 18 months. Foreign drug dealers would be beheaded. Chinese dealers would be strangled to death. In 1839 Lin wrote a letter to Queen Victoria asking her to help stop the opium trafficking. "The Way of Heaven [Tao] is fair to all. It does not allow us to harm others in order to benefit ourselves," he wrote. "All opium discovered in China will be cast into burning oil and destroyed. Any foreign ships that in the future arrive with opium on board will be set on fire." The letter concluded with a warning to the Queen: "Do not say you have not been warned. On receiving this, I hope Your Majesty will inform me immediately on the steps that have been taken at each of your ports to stop your opium trading."

Soon 1600 residents of the Canton province – dealers and drug addicts were arrested, and 42,000 opium pipes were destroyed. 14,000 chests of opium were seized. But 20,000 chests of opium were still on foreign ships anchored by the coast of China. Lin told foreign traders to turn the ships around, or else. The traders didn't take his threats seriously. Then Chinese troops surrounded the British Chamber of Commerce, as well as American and Indian opium traders' "factories" (trading post buildings) in Guangzhou. All Chinese servants who cooked and cleaned for the foreigners were ordered to leave.

To keep the pressure on the foreign traders inside the "factories," the Chinese made enormous noise using huge gongs day and night, and ran military drills under the foreigners' windows. Chinese workers sealed the entrances and exits to the traders' buildings with bricks. To communicate between the buildings the foreigners bribed Chinese servants to carry messages hidden in their shoes. The foreigners had no food and were allowed only two buckets of water a day. None of them knew how to cook or clean, and with the Chinese servants gone, the buildings were filthy and overrun with rats. To amuse themselves, the opium traders organized rat hunts.

Finally, the British Chief Superintendent of Trade in China gave in to the pressure and ordered the British to surrender their stock of opium – 1.15 million kilograms. He promised the Brits that their government would compensate them for the loss.

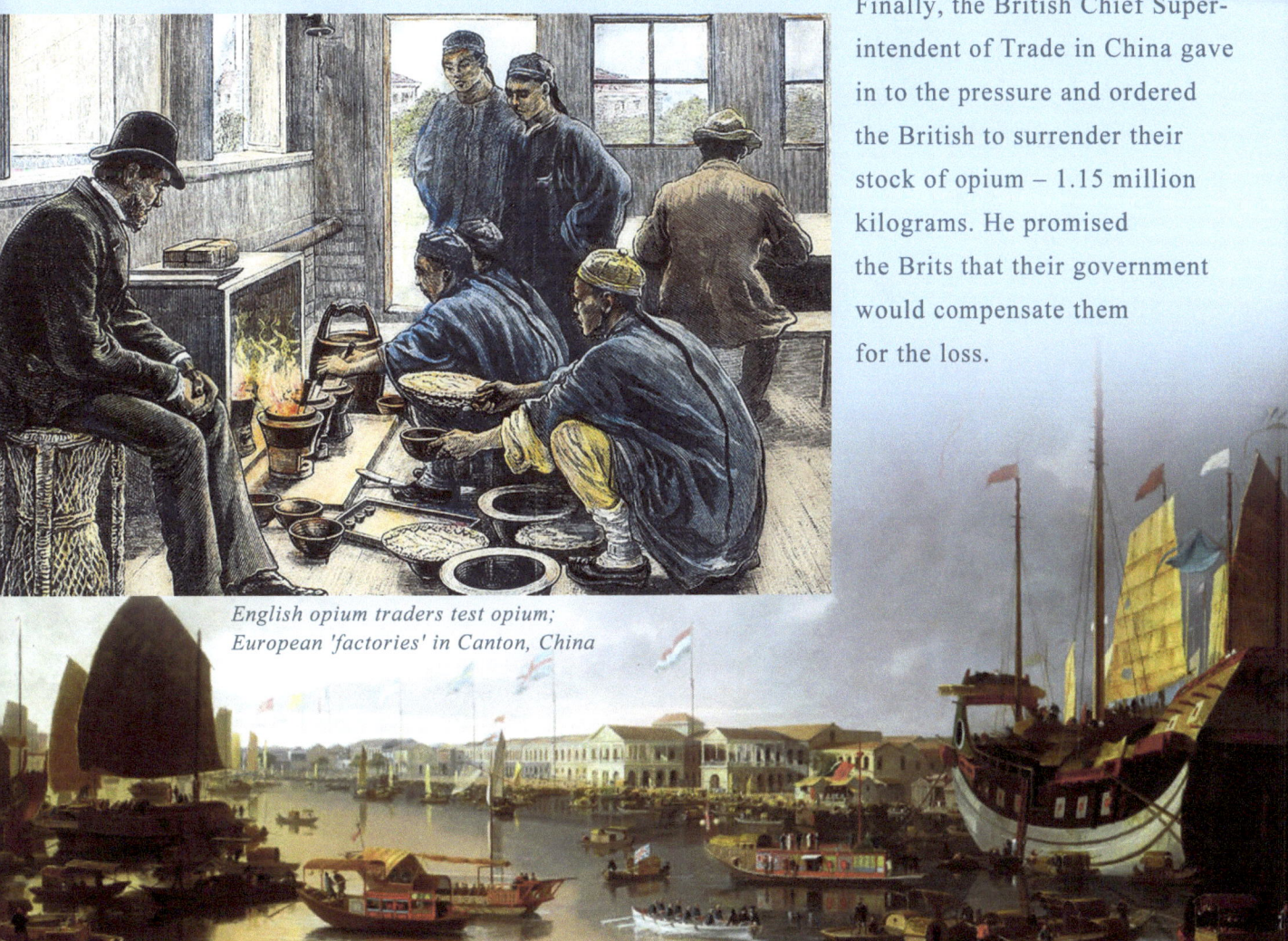

English opium traders test opium; European 'factories' in Canton, China

Lin Zexu rewarded him by sending 250 cows to the hungry Brits. Next American and Indian opium traders surrendered their opium and were told to leave China and never come back. The emperor sent Lin a gift of venison (deer meat) – a special sign indicating an upcoming promotion to a higher rank in the government, and a scroll of calligraphy created by the emperor himself. The scroll read, "Good luck and long life." To destroy the opium, Lin Zexu had 3 "pools" dug on the beach and lined with wood. The "cakes" of opium were crushed and dumped into the pools to dissolve. From the pools the dissolved opium flowed into the ocean to be dispersed by the currents.

Meanwhile in London opium traders paid journalists to stir up public opinion with lies about starvation, imprisonment, torture and executions of European traders in China. British newspapers lied about Lin, saying that he had seized the opium in order to enrich himself, and openly called for war. Opium traders wanted the military might of the British empire to back their business and looked for ways to provoke the war. In July 1839, British and American sailors in Hong Kong, enraged at the Chinese authorities who had arrested one of them, got drunk on rice wine and beat up local Chinese villagers. One of the villagers was killed. Lin Zexu demanded that the British surrender the murderers to the Chinese government. The British refused. In October Lin sent a fleet of 30 ships to expel the British ships from Hong Kong. That gave opium dealers a chance to finally provoke a military clash. Two British ships approached the Chinese fleet and opened fire. Chinese ship cannons couldn't aim well at close range and kept shooting way over the masts of the British ships. In a very short time the British sank 4 Chinese ships. The rest of the Chinese fleet sailed away.

In 1840 battles between Chinese and British ships became common. But the Chinese were so far behind in terms of military technology, they had no chance of stopping the British. British navy ships protected merchant vessels carrying opium, and the opium trade flourished again.

The British attack on the Chinese fleet, 1843

Lin Zexu tried to intimidate the Europeans. An Englishman who worked as a tutor to a British merchant's kids was kidnapped and thrown in jail. A French missionary who violated the Chinese law against missionary work, was publicly executed. In response, the British sent a powerful fleet of war steamships to teach Lin a lesson. While Lin did a lot to prepare the South of China for defense, the governors of provinces up north did nothing. So the British fleet sailed up the coast and captured Dinghai in the Zhejiang province of China. The emperor was furious and blamed Lin Zexu for provoking the war. Lin was fired and exiled to Xinjiang in Chinese Central Asia. For 5 years Lin lived in Xinjiang, writing poetry and studying the customs and culture of Central Asians. In 1845 the emperor forgave Lin and appointed him again a governor of a province.

Lin Zexu's fierce fight against opium trade is celebrated in art, poetry, novels and movies – in China and in Chinese communities around the world. There is a small planet named Lin Zexu. A statue of Lin Zexu stands in New York City's Chinatown. The inscription on its base reads, "Pioneer in the war against drugs."

The First Opium War ended with the Treaty of Nanking (Nanjing) in 1842. The treaty made Hong Kong a British colony and obligated China to pay *reparations* (compensation) for the destroyed opium. The Second Opium War (1856-1860) was even more disastrous for China. In 1856, Chinese authorities seized a British cargo ship, and arrested its Chinese sailors. They believed that some of the sailors were pirates. The British had been looking for a pretext to resume the Opium Wars in order to force the Chinese

19th-century magazine illustrations depicting the Opium Wars

to make opium trade legal. So a joint British and French force landed in China and shelled Canton. As they made their way toward Beijing, the Qing government took a few British and French diplomats hostage. They were tortured and some were killed. In retaliation (revenge), once the European armies took Beijing, British commander Lord Elgin ordered the troops to loot and burn the historic imperial Old Summer Palace, Yuan Ming Yuan. 300 servants and court ladies perished in the flames. Precious art and centuries-worth of cultural treasures stored in the palace were gone within hours. The Chinese government signed a treaty making opium trade legal, giving the Western powers control of its ports, and agreeing to pay more reparations. The period between 1839 and 1949 – from the First Opium War to the establishment of the People's Republic of China – is often referred to in China as the **Century of Humiliation**. During this period China lost control over large portions of its territory and suffered from invasions and a civil war.

Ruins of the Old Summer Palace, a photo of a sedan chair, China, 1870; The Anglo-French fleet in Hong Kong, 1860, prior to the assault on Beijing

Sedan Chair

Sedan chairs carried on poles were used by Chinese aristocracy and government officials throughout Chinese history. In the 19th century they became a form of street transportation similar to a taxi. The English word 'sedan' came from the Italian language. It traces to Latin 'sedere' = to sit.

Empress Dowager Cixi

1835 – 1908

Empress Cixi (pronounced 'Tsi-shi') was born into the family of a mid-level government official belonging to a noble Manchu clan. It was the era of the Manchurian Qing Dynasty, when hundreds of thousands of Manchus moved to Beijing from Manchuria, and all the top positions in the government and at the imperial court were controlled by Manchu clans. These newcomers had little respect for the system of Imperial Examinations. They bought their ranks and titles from corrupt officials – and kept the Han Chinese out of the government. When Cixi was 18, she became one of the wives of the 21-year-old Xianfeng Emperor of the Qing Dynasty. But of all his wives, she was the only one who gave birth to a boy. Suddenly she was the most honored and important woman in the palace. And she had yet one more advantage: Being Manchu, the Emperor's wives couldn't read or write Chinese. Cixi was the only one who could. She helped the Xianfeng Emperor read government reports, and even wrote his comments on them.

Xianfeng was entirely uninterested in governing his empire, plus, as a heavy opium smoker, he had a problem focusing on anything. Cixi's enthusiasm for government work was a blessing to him. After a few years of this work, Cixi learned everything about the structure and functions of each government department and could potentially run the government herself. That's what made Cixi the power behind the throne that ruled China for half a century.

In 1860, when Beijing was captured by British and French troops and the Summer Palace was burned and looted, the Xianfeng Emperor and his family fled Beijing.

A French magazine cartoon: Britain, Germany, Russia, and France divide China.

And that wasn't all. The *Taiping Rebellion* – an anti-Manchu revolt that flared up in 1850 – kept going strong, sweeping over the whole of south China. Unable to cope with so much bad news, the emperor fell into depression, overdosed on alcohol and opium, and died a year later. Cixi's 5-year-old son Zaichun inherited the throne.

Cixi, 26 years old, was given the title Dowager Empress, but the role of a *regent* (a person who runs the government while the monarch is a kid) was awarded to a 'regency council' of 8 ministers. Cixi didn't like that. And having already mastered the art of palace intrigues and political back-stabbing, she conspired with some Qing princes to overthrow the 'regency council.' With fake documents and lying "witnesses" she had the 8 council ministers accused of treason and arrested. Three of them were executed. Others were pardoned to show how "merciful" the empress was. Now Cixi was the regent ruling China from "behind the curtain." The "curtain" wasn't just a political term. It was a real curtain. Since women were not allowed to get involved in politics, empress dowagers sat behind a curtain next to kid emperors during court receptions and government councils.

Taiping rebellion

The Taiping uprising started as a peasant rebellion and turned into an anti-Manchu revolt by the Han Chinese. Natural disasters and heavy taxes ruined Chinese farmers. Some left their villages and formed bands of robbers. Others formed *militias* (self-defense units) to protect themselves from robbers and pirates. The government was extremely corrupt and of no help. Over time various militias and rebel groups joined forces. The leader of the uprising was Hong Xiuquan, a scholar from a poor family of Hakka, a minority ethnic group in southern China. Hong failed the Imperial Examination 4 times and ended up in such a state of despair and depression that many thought he had lost his mind. Suddenly, he started having visions. Trying to interpret them, he studied the Bible with American Christian missionaries and came to the conclusion that he was the brother of Jesus Christ, and that God had commanded him to fight the demons – the Qing government.

Hong's rebels, who called themselves the Taiping Heavenly Kingdom, protected farmers from bandits and Qing tax collectors, and their numbers grew. Women fought alongside men. In 1851, armed with only pikes and axes, the rebels clashed with the government troops and won.

Hong Xiuquan

The territory they controlled was expanding. From a few thousand peasants the uprising grew to 1 million fighters. One of the reasons they kept winning against the Qing army was the rebels' ban on opium. 90% of soldiers in the imperial troops were opium addicts. No wonder they were losing. In 1853 the rebels seized Nanjing. Soon, however, the tide turned: Their own leaders started fighting among themselves. Hong now lived in a luxurious house in Nanjing, had servants and a bunch of wives. His followers didn't like that. Also the fact that he rejected Confucian values and traditional Chinese culture was a problem for many around him. Eventually the Qing army got their act together and started winning. In 1864 it besieged Nanjing. The rebels defending the city ran out of food. They ended up eating wild plants and mushrooms. Hong Xiuquan died of food poisoning, and Nanjing fell a month later. The Taiping rebellion was the most destructive civil war in the history of the world. Almost 30 million people (up to 10% of China's population at that time) perished in battles or were killed by famines.

The "dragon robe"

The "dragon robe" embroidered with dragon images was the uniform of Chinese court officials during the Qing dynasty. The number of dragon's claws indicated the wearer's rank. Five-clawed dragons appeared exclusively on the emperor's clothes.

To weaken the Manchu aristocracy that despised her, Empress Cixi gave many top government and military positions to the Han Chinese. She also realized that China had fallen behind the Western world. It was time to "learn from foreigners." Many factories were modernized and education was improved. The empress opened a school where kids studied technology and foreign languages – English, French, and Russian – and many students were sent to colleges abroad. But as they came home, they brought with them ideas that were so unacceptable to Cixi, that the "learn from foreigners" program was shut down. Empress Cixi also grew extremely suspicious of any technology. She resisted building railroads because she thought they were too noisy and could "disturb the tombs of the emperors." And when she finally gave her permission for the first railroad project, she demanded that train cars be pulled by horses to avoid all that noise! Riding in a car was also out of the question, because the driver sat at the same level as the empress, not below her, as custom required.

Things didn't go well with Empress Cixi's son Zaichun, either. He hated school work, and at age 16 could hardly read. At 17 he married a princess whose grandpa was one of the regency council ministers who had been executed by his mom! Plus the princess' Zodiac sign was 'tiger,' while Cixi's sign was 'goat' – so the empress believed her son's wife would seek to destroy her. To keep her son away from his wife's influence, Cixi ordered him to live alone and complete his studies. Instead, the prince escaped from the palace dressed as a common citizen, and had fun with his friends in some of the most dangerous neighborhoods of Beijing. Zaichun died at 20, in 1875, from smallpox. Cixi chose her 4-year-old nephew, Zaitian, to be crowned the new emperor and continued ruling China "from behind the curtain." In 1889, when Zaitian turned 18, Cixi declared that she would retire from political life and let the emperor rule on his own, but nobody believed her – including herself. She ran a network of spies and advisors who helped her control the government, and public opinion.

In 1894 a China-Japan war broke out and the Qing Dynasty lost Taiwan to Japan. Zaitian, now the Guangxu Emperor, decided to modernize China's economy, society, and government to stop poverty, corruption, and humiliating military defeats. But Cixi suspected that the emperor was acting under the influence of foreigners – maybe the British or even the Japanese. So Zaitian's advisors were beheaded, their reforms canceled and the emperor was locked up on an island in the middle of the lake in the Forbidden City. But Zaitian was right: Without economic and social reforms, China was growing weaker and weaker. Meanwhile, another massive disaster loomed ahead – the **Boxer Rebellion**.

Chinese court ladies – a 19th-century photograph

THE BOXER REBELLION

The Boxer Rebellion was an uprising against the foreign invaders and Christian missionaries who were given special privileges in China by the treaties that ended the Opium Wars. Some missionaries seized Buddhist temples and turned them into Christian churches – which led to riots. Others shielded Chinese Christians from police and courts, so criminals converted to Christianity and evaded justice, causing wide-spread anger. The rebellion was started by a secret society, the Society of Righteous and Harmonious Fists, which became known as "the Boxers" because it encouraged its members to learn and practice martial arts. The Boxers attacked factories, railroads, and other properties of British and French companies. They also hunted down and murdered Christian missionaries and their students. Empress Cixi supported the Boxers, viewing them as a patriotic movement – strong enough to repel the Western invaders. In 1900 the Boxers' army arrived in Beijing, and, along with Qing troops, laid siege to the Legation Quarter – an area where foreign embassies were located. About 1000 foreign diplomats and soldiers and 3000 Chinese Christians were sheltering in the quarter.

The siege and liberation of the Legation Quarter – French illustrated magazines, 1900

Empress Cixi ordered all diplomats to leave Beijing within 24 hours, but they refused, fearing that they would be murdered the moment they opened the gates. Only the German ambassador left the quarter and, indeed, he was immediately shot, in the street outside. In response, eight nations – the United States, Russia, Japan, Britain, France, Germany, Italy, and the Austro-Hungarian Empire – sent their troops to save the residents of the Legation Quarter. The invading force was many times smaller than the armies of the Boxers and the Qing Dynasty, but its weapons and tactics were far more advanced. In the years prior to the rebellion the Qing government had set aside a lot of money to modernize their army, but Cixi believed rebuilding the Summer Palace was more important. The funds meant for the army had been spent on the palace restoration and decor.

During the siege, many diplomats and refugees in the quarter perished. Especially deadly were the mines planted by the Chinese troops in the tunnels they dug under the quarter. The Boxers also used the "Anaconda tactic." They built barricades around the quarter and thickened them by a few brick rows a day, advancing a few feet closer to the quarter every day. The foreigners fought back with rifles, 3 machine guns, and one cannon named "The International Gun" because its barrel was British, its wheels were Italian, the shells were Russian, and the artillery men who operated it were from the United States. Russian and American marines attempted a few joint counterattacks on the Boxers, but achieved very little. Finally after 55 days of the siege, the 50 thousand-strong Eight-Nation army fought its way to Beijing, defeated the Chinese imperial troops and the Boxers, and freed the Legation Quarter.

Chinese volunteers join the rebel army

When the Eight-Nation army fighting the Boxers reached Beijing, the Qing court including Cixi and her nephew, the Guangxu Emperor, fled. Cixi dressed as a Buddhist nun and even cut off her 6-inch nails to hide her identity. Guangxu's wife dared to suggest that fleeing their own capital in the middle of the night was shameful. For that she was tossed into a well and drowned in front of her husband. Her death was announced to her family as a "patriotic suicide."
In the end, the Qing government had to sign capitulation treaties with the invaders – pay more reparations and agree to the presence of foreign troops in Beijing.

When the imperial court returned to Beijing, Cixi pretended she was grateful to the foreign troops for defeating the Boxers and started promoting government reforms. She even installed electric lights in the Forbidden City and talked about introducing constitutional monarchy. But her life was close to its end, and most of these reforms were never implemented.
In December of 1908 she poisoned her nephew, the Guangxu Emperor, and gave the throne to his 3-year-old nephew Puyi. But Cixi's hope of ruling as a regent for another 15 years was not to be fulfilled. She died the very next day, of dysentery. Puyi was the last emperor of China. Three years later, in 1912, the Xinhai Revolution overthrew the Qing Dynasty and established the Republic of China.

Photo: Empress Cixi walking in a garden

Feng Shui

Based on the Taoist idea of Chi (life force), Feng Shui is an ancient Chinese art of establishing harmony between man-made structures and the environment. It advises where to construct buildings, where to place rooms in buildings, as well as where to place windows, doors, and objects inside rooms in ways that create a sense of balance. "Feng" means "wind," and "shui" means "water." Feng Shui developed from an ancient form of divination (predicting the future) by observing the patterns found in nature – rock and sand formations, directions of wind and water currents. Modern Feng Shui mostly deals with architecture and interior design, teaching where to place furniture, plants, mirrors, and other objects in relation to doors, windows and cardinal directions. For example, Feng Shui experts say the best spot in a room (where your desk or bed should be) is the farthest from the door, with a clear line of sight to the door, but not directly in front of the door.

*In the 19th century Feng Shui became increasingly popular in China. It was viewed as a native spiritual practice and a form of protest against both Western and Manchurian cultures. The anti-Manchu rebels of the Taiping Revolt and the Boxers embraced Feng Shui as one of the features of Chinese national identity.
The Qing government tried to suppress it, but failed.*

Sun Yat-sen
1866 – 1925

Sun Yat-sen was a Chinese revolutionary whose work led to the overthrow of the Qing Dynasty. He is often called the "Father of Modern China." Sun Yat-sen was born into a family of Hakka and Cantonese villagers from Canton Province (now Guangdong). They owned some land, but not enough for farming. Sun Yat-sen's dad worked as a tailor and a porter. As a kid Sun Yat-sen loved listening to the accounts of battles and adventures told by his old neighbor, a soldier who had participated in the Taiping Rebellion. The story of a handful of rebels who turned into a vast revolutionary army and seized the entire south of China in less than 3 years became an inspiration for his future revolutionary work.

In 1878 Sun Yat-sen's elder brother Sun Mei came home from Hawaii where he had stayed for a few years. It turned out Sun Mei was earning a good living in Hawaii. He owned and ran a small rice plantation and a village general store. Sun Mei brought enough money home with him to rebuild his parents' house, and invited Sun Yat-sen to come live with him in Honolulu. Their parents were against it, but 14-year-old Sun Yat-sen had his brother buy him a ticket on a British ship carrying Chinese *indentured laborers* to the sugar plantations in Hawaii, and boarded the ship without his parents permission. Years later Sun Yat-sen recalled his very first encounter with Western culture on board the British ship. One of the British sailors died. His body was placed in a sack and covered with the British **Union Jack** flag. The crew rang the bells, the captain said a prayer, and the sailor's body was lowered into the ocean. Sun Yat-sen was struck with the simplicity of this burial in comparison with traditional Chinese funeral ceremonies that required many elaborate rituals.

Indentured Laborers

*Indentured labor is a work governed by a contract (called an "indenture") where a person agrees to work for a period of time without being paid. Only food and shelter are provided. Many European and Asian immigrants to the United States and European colonies signed these contracts to pay off their debts, or in exchange for a ticket to a ship that would take them to a new land. Large numbers of Chinese workers (nicknamed **coolies** from the Hindi 'kuli' – 'wages') came to the US and the Caribbean to work on plantations, railroads, and various construction projects. Many of them were tricked into signing indentured labor contracts they didn't understand, and worked in appalling conditions for years.*

Sun Yat-sen lived in Honolulu for 4 years. He went to a British school where he studied English, math, physics, and other subjects, but his favorite subject was Bible studies. At 18 Sun Yat-sen became a Christian and was baptized, but when he tried to explain the Ten Commandments to his brother, Sun Mei was upset and complained to their parents that Sun Yat-sen had lost respect for his ancestors, fallen under Western influence, and should be sent back to China. Sun Yat-sen came home to Canton and that's where his "Western" views really got him into big trouble. During a religious festival he walked into a local temple, climbed on top of a statue representing a divine being worshiped in their village and addressed his neighbors with these words: "Give me a single reason for worshiping this idol! Is it good to you? Can it protect you? How can you kneel in front of an idol who cannot even protect itself?" Having said that, Sun Yat-sen broke off the arm of the statue! The punishment for a crime like this was... beheading. Only because his dad was much respected in the village, the villagers agreed to let Sun Yat-sen go, as long as he left Canton with only the clothes he wore and never came back. Sun Yat-sen ended up in Hong Kong. Supported by money secretly sent to him by his family, he studied medicine, became a surgeon, got married, and had a son.

Chinese immigrants aboard the steamship "Alaska" on their way to San Francisco, 1876

All day he performed surgery at a hospital. Every night he spent with his friends, members of many secret revolutionary societies of Hong Kong. In 1894 Sun Yat-sen founded his own revolutionary group, the Revive China Society. Two years later the revolutionaries were ready for their first attempt at an armed uprising – in the city of Guangzhou. In secret workshops, they manufactured hundreds of bombs. Guns and dynamite were smuggled into Guangzhou from the Philippines. One of the revolutionaries, Lu Haodong designed a flag for the rebel army that featured the twelve-ray sun on a blue sky. He told the tailors who were sewing the flags these were bed sheets for his little sister, and that the sun represented "family love throughout the 12 hours of the day and the 12 months of the year." But on the eve of the uprising the revolutionaries found out that they had been betrayed. Now the government knew the location of their headquarters. Realizing that their secret society membership book with detailed information on every participant of the uprising remained at the headquarters, Lu Haodong rushed there and burned the book. But a few minutes later the police broke in and arrested him. He was publicly beheaded. Now every wall in Canton displayed posters announcing a reward for the capture of Sun Yat-sen. Sun Yat-sen escaped to Hong Kong. To conceal his identity, he cut off his queue, grew a mustache and wore a European suit hoping to pass for a Japanese businessman. In 1896 he came to London on the invitation of his teacher, British surgeon Dr. James Cantlie.

The Queue

The queue was a male hairstyle that came to China from Manchuria during the Qing Dynasty. Hair on top of the head was grown long and braided while the sides of the head were shaved. All men in China were required to wear a queue. The queue eventually became a symbol of oppression and national shame.

Lu Haodong's flag and a magazine illustration "The Chinese cut off their queues," 1911

By this time Sun Yat-sen was famous in revolutionary circles, and the Qing police hunted him relentlessly. While he was still on the ship on his way to London, the Chinese were already demanding that the British government arrest and send him to China as an especially dangerous political criminal. Ironically, Dr. Cantlie lived almost next door to the Chinese Legation (embassy) in London. "Don't go near it! They'll grab you and ship you off to China!" he warned Sun Yat-sen. One morning on his way to church, Sun Yat-sen was approached by a Chinese man who struck a friendly conversation with him. A few moments later, two more Chinese men suddenly appeared at his side. They seized Sun Yat-sen and dragged him up the steps into a building – the Chinese Legation! He was locked in a room and constantly watched.

Now a prisoner, Sun Yat-sen tore his handkerchief and wrote desperate messages – appeals for help – on pieces of the cloth. He wrapped them around coins and threw them out the barred window. "My despair was complete, and only by prayers to God could I gain any comfort... If I didn't have the hope given to me by prayer, I would've gone mad," he wrote in a book describing this event, *Kidnapped in London*. Sun Yat-sen begged one of the English servants who brought him food to help him. "My life is entirely in your hands," he said. "If you let this matter be known outside, I shall be saved. If not, I shall certainly be bound and beheaded. It is in your hands whether my life is saved or taken from me. Would you be faithful to God or to your master?" The servant agreed to help. Dr. Cantlie found a message by his door, "There is a friend of yours imprisoned in the Chinese Legation. They intend to send him to China, where it is certain they will hang him." Panicking, Dr. Cantlie started calling police and his acquaintances at the British Foreign Office, but it was a Sunday and nobody was at work. And on Monday, when everyone returned to their offices, none of the British officials seemed to be interested in the fate of a Chinese revolutionary.

In desperation Dr. Cantlie asked the Globe newspaper to publish Sun Yat-sen's story. In the evening newspaper sellers on every corner of London shouted out the headlines: "Chinese revolutionary kidnapped in London!" "Shanghai-ed in London!" Instantly, a crowd of reporters and sensation-seekers gathered in front of the Chinese Legation building looking into the windows and shouting questions for the Chinese diplomats. The scandal reached the British Secretary for Foreign Affairs. He stated that imprisonment without trial was incompatible with British law, and advised the Chinese to let their prisoner go. Sun Yat-sen was released and by the time he returned to his hotel, there was a crowd of reporters waiting for him. He was now a celebrity – a hero in the fight for freedom.

To "shanghai"

The verb "to shanghai" came into common use in English at the end of the 19th century. Ship owners in the Chinese seaport of Shanghai often kidnapped men to force them to work on ships making long voyages. A person could be drugged or knocked unconscious and would wake up on a ship in the middle of the ocean.

One day, in the British Museum library reading room, Sun Yat-sen met some Russian revolutionaries. Among them was Vladimir Lenin, their future leader. The Russians asked him, "How long will it take for the Chinese Revolution to succeed?" "Perhaps 30 years," answered Sun Yat-sen. The Russians seemed very surprised. "So, what about the revolution in Russia? How long do you need to succeed?" asked Sun Yat-sen. "If we could succeed in 100 years, we'd be happy," was the answer. It was 1897 – only 14 years to the 1911 revolution that swept away the Qing dynasty in China... and only 20 years to the 1917 Russian revolution that shattered the Russian Empire.

In 1905 Sun Yat-sen built the Chinese Revolutionary Alliance in Tokyo. Its goal was "to expel the Tatar barbarians (the Manchus), to revive Chinese civilization, to establish a republic, and to distribute land equally among the people." The Alliance launched 4 armed revolts, none of which succeeded. To raise money for the revolution in China, Sun Yat-sen wanted to go to the United States. But the mood in the US was extremely anti-Chinese. Following the disastrous Opium Wars, hundreds of thousands of Chinese immigrants flooded the US cities. They were blamed for rising crime and falling wages in America. As a result, the Chinese Exclusion Act of 1882 completely prohibited immigration from China to the United States. To get around this law, Sun Yat-sen bought a fake birth certificate saying he had been born in Hawaii. He was lucky: they let him into the US.

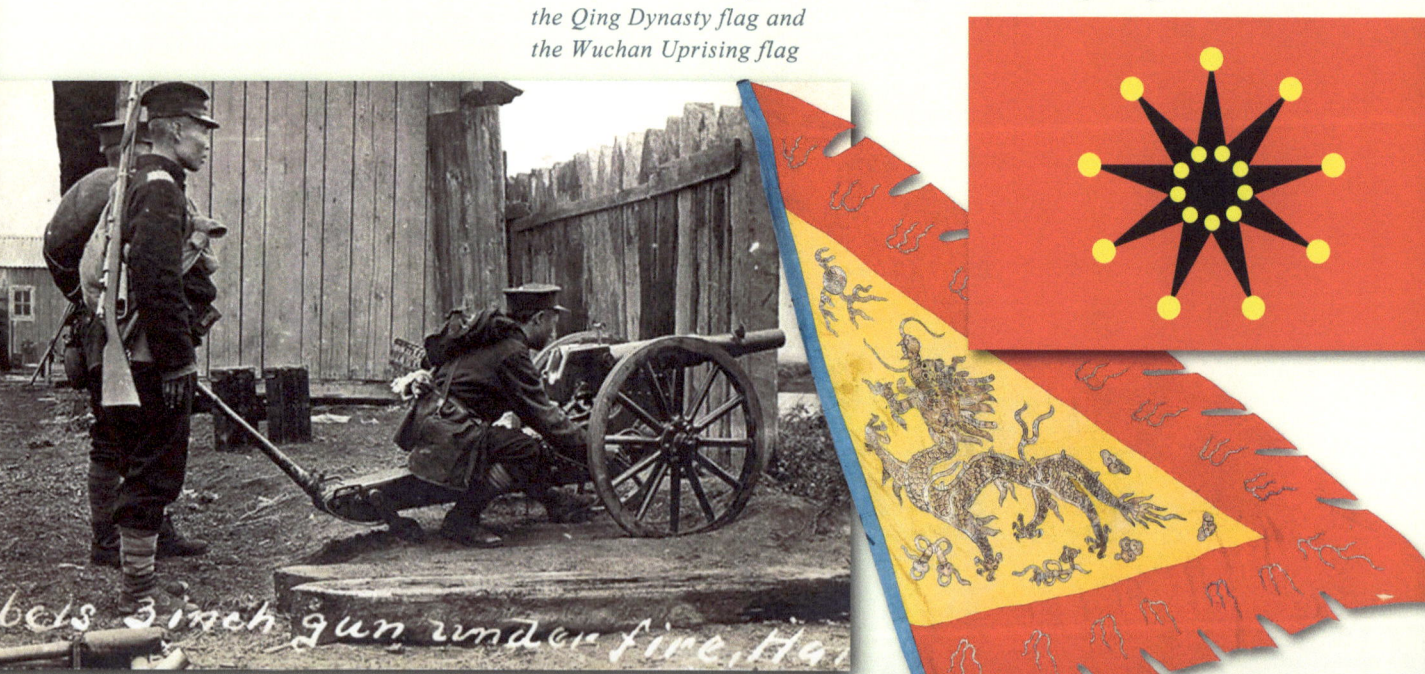

Chinese revolutionary soldiers during the Wuchan Uprising; the Qing Dynasty flag and the Wuchan Uprising flag

In the Chinatowns of San Francisco and New York, Chinese laundrymen, gardeners, and laborers listened to Sun Yat-sen and donated their savings to defeat the Qing Empire. Sun Yat-sen later recalled a "donation" given to him by a poor laundry worker. The man knocked on Sun Yat-sen's door, handed him a cloth bag, and left. The bag contained cash – all of the man's life's savings. In 1911 the Qing government granted foreign companies the right to build and operate railways in China. This caused mass protests and prompted the Chinese Revolutionary Alliance to launch an uprising in Wuhan, the second largest city in China after Shanghai. On October 9, 1911, an explosion occurred at a secret workshop in Wuhan where the revolutionaries were making bombs. The local government began arresting them. But the Qing military officers who had been ordered to hunt down the rebels, changed sides and joined the Revolutionary Alliance fighters. Together they attacked the government armory, occupied a large portion of Wuhan and established their own Military Government.

As the news of the revolutionaries' success in Wuhan spread, 14 provinces of China declared independence from the Qing Empire. In early October, while still in the US, Sun Yat-sen received a coded telegram from Hong Kong, but his notebook with the keys to decode the telegram had been sent with his luggage to Denver, Colorado. When he finally decoded it days later, he was surprised to read, "Urgently need money. Preparations for the uprising have been completed." The next morning the newspaper headlines announced the revolution in China. As Sun Yat-sen was traveling home, in Singapore, huge crowds gathered on the pier to see him. It had become known that the revolutionary organizations chose him to be the first president of the Republic of China. People threw flowers at his feet, and photographers hurried to take his pictures.

Sun Yat-sen was sworn in as the first president of the Republic of China in Nanjing on January 1, 1912. In February the last Qing emperor, 6-year-old Puyi, abdicated (quit) the throne putting an end to the history of imperial China that had lasted for over 2,000 years. Two months later, because of infighting among the revolutionaries, Sun Yat-sen had to resign and left for Japan. China entered the so-called "Warlord Era," with different regions of China setting up their own military governments. For years, Sun Yat-sen struggled to unify the revolutionaries once again. He eventually managed to bring together their two main forces – the ***Kuomintang*** (Chinese Nationalist Party, or ***KMT***) led by Sun Yat-sen (and, later, Chiang Kai-shek), and the ***Chinese Communist Party (CCP)***, founded in 1921. Sun Yat-sen died of illness in 1925. After his death the communists and the nationalists split and parted ways which eventually led to an 18-year-long civil war – won by the communists.

EMPEROR PUYI

1906 – 1967

When the Chinese Revolution overthrew the Qing Dynasty, 6-year-old Puyi was not informed that his empire had turned into the Republic of China. He lived in the imperial palace in the Forbidden City surrounded by servants and tutors, and the republic continued to pay all his expenses! The reason for this generosity became clear in 1915 when President Yuan of the Republic of China (who replaced Sun Yat-sen) suddenly proclaimed himself emperor and moved into the Forbidden City imperial palace! Turned out he had planned it all along, but, while waiting for the right moment, he kept Puyi as a "placeholder" to preserve the imperial court for himself. Yuan's plan, however, failed. He had no public support, and soon stepped down. In 1917 one of the former Qing Dynasty generals staged a revolt and tried to return the imperial powers to 11-year-old Puyi. But the supporters of the republic had a Chinese pilot drop 3 bombs on the Forbidden City. It was the first ever attack by the Chinese air force. The pro-empire revolt was defeated.

A vintage print "The Emperor of China sledging on the lake in the palace gardens"; Puyi and his wife Wanrong

Describing life in the imperial palace in his autobiography, Puyi wrote, "Whenever I went for a stroll in the garden a whole procession had to be organized." The procession included servants carrying a silk canopy to protect the emperor from the sun, chairs, umbrellas, and changes of clothes. Next came officials of the Imperial Tea Department carrying boxes of cakes, pastries, and tea service. They were followed by the palace Medical Department, carrying cases of medicines and first-aid equipment. "This procession of several dozen people walked in perfect silence and order." Every meal was served on 7 tables: "Usually there were two tables of main dishes and another one with warmers for hot dishes in winter. There were three tables with cakes, rice, and porridge, and there was another small table of salted vegetables. Food was served on imperial yellow porcelain with dragon designs and the words "Ten thousand long lives without limit." In winter I ate from silver dishes placed on top of porcelain bowls of hot water. Every dish or bowl had a strip of silver on it as a precaution against poison." After the young emperor finished his meal, a servant was sent with a report to his grandmother and other relatives: "Your slave reports to his masters: The Lord of Ten Thousand Years consumed one bowl of rice and meat, one pancake, and a bowl of congee (rice porridge). He consumed it with delight." If the kid emperor threw a tantrum, the head of his household issued the order: "The Lord of Ten Thousand Years has fire in his heart. Let him sing for a while to disperse it." The emperor was locked in a room and kept there until he stopped crying.

Silver and poison

In the Middle Ages silver was used to detect poison because silver enters into a chemical reaction with the sulphur present in some poisonous substances, such as arsenic sulfide. As a result of this reaction, silver tarnishes (darkens), forming a black compound, silver sulfide, Ag_2S. A sudden appearance of black discoloration on silver spoons or goblets signaled the presence of poison – but only if it contained sulphur. You can observe this chemical reaction if you eat an egg with a silver or silver-plated spoon, since egg yolks are rich in sulphur.

Puyi, the child emperor

As Puyi was growing up he studied world history and English, and started writing and publishing poetry. He got himself a telephone and called random numbers in Beijing just to experience the excitement of hearing real voices on the other end. "I rang up a Beijing opera actor, and an acrobat, and hung up without saying who I was," he later recalled. "I called up a restaurant and ordered a meal to be sent to a false address."

Puyi and Wanrong; Puyi on a Manchukuo stamp

He also planned to escape from the palace and leave for England, but his British tutor rejected that plan. At 17 he married a Manchu princess named Wanrong. Two years later the new government of the Republic of China kicked him out of the Forbidden City, and he moved to a Japanese-occupied neighborhood in the Chinese city of Tianjin. He lived in luxury, wasting enormous amounts of money shopping. His money came from selling off treasures of the Forbidden City palaces to antique dealers.

In 1931 Puyi asked the Japanese Minister of War to help him restore the Qing Empire and return to its throne. The Japanese had been planning an invasion anyway. Puyi's participation was an opportunity to turn "invasion" into the "restoration of the empire." Japanese troops attacked Northeast China and occupied Manchuria. Hiding in the trunk of a car, Puyi left for Manchuria where he was soon proclaimed the emperor of the Japanese "puppet state" Manchukuo. China declared Puyi a traitor. In Manchuria he discovered that as the "ruler" of a Japanese colony, he was actually a prisoner. The Japanese didn't allow him to leave his "palace" – the former Salt Tax office. His "puppet" government officials, servants, and people in the streets – both the Manchus and the Chinese – could hardly hide their scorn for him. His wife Wanrong hated the Japanese and despised Puyi for being a traitor to China. Behind his back she put on sunglasses (Puyi always wore sunglasses) and performed comedy skits mocking Puyi in front of his servants. Puyi responded by brutally beating his servants for every misstep and starving them in the basement.

Puyi's biographer Edward Behr described the emperor's daily routine: "He did not get up until noon, ate lunch at two, and then promptly went back to bed for a nap. He played tennis in the afternoon in summer, or table tennis indoors in winter, and rode a bicycle on the grounds of his palace compound for exercise. He would sometimes get behind the wheel of his Buick, and drive it a few hundred yards round and round the palace. He had a large collection of Chinese opera records, which he listened to for hours on end." Meanwhile, one million Chinese peasants were enslaved every year and forced to work in Japanese factories in Manchuria producing weapons and ammunition for Japan. Their farms and land were seized and taken away from them by thousands of Japanese settlers who had moved to Manchuria.

In 1940 during Puyi's trip to Japan, he was informed that the Emperor of Japan expected him to abandon Confucianism and adopt Shinto (the Japanese state religion) as the religion of the puppet state of Manchukuo. Saying "no" was out of the question. Japanese Emperor Hirohito handed Puyi three symbols of Shinto: a piece of jade, a sword, and a bronze mirror. "What was that? Beijing antique shops are full of such trinkets... I burst into tears on the drive back," Puyi recalled in his autobiography. Now even he, himself, despised his role as a fake puppet emperor. The Japanese built hundreds of Shinto temples all around Manchuria and forced Manchurians to bow down to them. It was a serious blunder that drove the native population of Manchuria to the verge of rioting.

Throughout World War II Puyi believed that Nazi Germany and Japan were winning. His Japanese handlers didn't allow him to read any newspapers or tune into radio broadcasts that reported the truth. When Japan suffered defeats, Japanese journalists called them "heroic sacrifices" and presented them as victories. In his autobiography *From Emperor to Citizen* Puyi recalled making a speech at a Japanese military ceremony honoring "human bullets" – **kamikaze** soldiers (soldiers who volunteered to go on suicide missions). "The dozen or so victims were drawn up in a line in front of me. I finished the speech, and only then did I notice that their faces were grey and tears were flowing down their cheeks. I heard some of them sobbing." Puyi's Japanese advisor told him the soldiers cried because they were moved by his speech. But Puyi knew that was a lie. He recalled thinking, "You're frightened that I've glimpsed what your 'human bullets' really feel. Well, if you're frightened, I'm terrified."

Japanese propaganda poster: Friendship of the Manchu, the Han Chinese, and the Japanese in Manchukuo

Puyi with Emperor Hirohito of Japan during his visit to Japan in 1935

In the summer of 1945 Puyi looked out his window and saw his Manchurian guards take off their uniforms and run away. That's when he found out that Nazi Germany had lost the war, that the Russians had occupied Berlin and invaded Manchuria, and that the Americans had burned the 6 largest Japanese cities with fire bombs. It took the Russians only 12 days to overrun Manchukuo. Escaping Manchuria on a train, Puyi saw hundreds of terrified Japanese colonists at every station trying to scramble on board. A few days later Puyi learned that the Americans had dropped atomic bombs on Hiroshima and Nagasaki, and that the Japanese Emperor Hirohito had proclaimed the surrender of Japan.

Puyi rushed to Shenyang where a Japanese plane was supposed to pick him up. But instead of the Japanese plane, a few Russian military aircraft landed on the airfield. A Russian assault unit seized the airport and captured Puyi and his Japanese advisors. On their way to Russian Siberia Puyi realized that he didn't want the Russians to view him as a Japanese collaborator. He approached the plane captain and said, "We don't want to be on the same plane with the Japanese war criminals!" The Russians understood him, and, during a refuelling stop, they moved his Japanese advisors onto a different plane.

Now in Siberia, Puyi lived at a beautiful resort hotel and was treated as a guest rather than as a prisoner. He was allowed to keep his servants who dressed him up, brushed his teeth, and made his bed. Russians didn't allow him to beat the servants, so he punished them by slapping them on the face instead. Puyi asked for political asylum, but his request was denied. China was now in the middle of a civil war between the army of the Republic of China under the command of Chiang Kai-shek and the forces of the Chinese Communist Party led by Mao Zedong. Chiang Kai-shek swore to execute Puyi and kept demanding that the Russians send the former emperor back to China. But the Soviet government said "No." They had already promised to hand Puyi over to the Chinese Communist Party once Chiang Kai-shek was defeated.

Puyi's wife Wanrong wasn't as fortunate. She was captured by Chinese guerillas and put on display at a local jail. People came to see the last empress of China, and weren't disappointed. Wanrong's mind had been blown out by opium addiction. She rushed around her cage

Puyi arrives in Russia

demanding more opium and ordering around imaginary servants. Having entirely lost her mind, she stopped eating and starved to death in her prison cell in 1946, at age 39. The same year Puyi was flown to Tokyo to be a witness at the international Tokyo War Crimes Tribunal. Over there he lied, saying he had never willingly agreed to be the puppet emperor in Manchuria, and insisted that he had all those years, been only a prisoner, of the Japanese.

In 1949 the Chinese Communist Party won the civil war and established the **People's Republic of China**. American military planes flew Chiang Kai-shek and the remnants of his army to Taiwan. Puyi was sent to China. He expected to be shot on arrival. Instead the new Chinese authorities met him warmly and explained to him that he would be sent to a prison camp for Japanese war criminals and Chiang Kai-shek's officials where he would be 're-educated' so one day, hopefully, he could sincerely embrace socialist and communist ideas. Indeed, the prison was a *re-education camp*. For the first time in his life Puyi had to tie his own shoelaces and brush his own teeth... Along with studying socialist political and economic theory, prisoners were taken on field trips. One of them was to Unit 731, the World War II Japanese biological weapons lab, where the Japanese had conducted atrocious experiments on people, killing over 14,000 Chinese soldiers and civilians, as well as many Russian prisoners of war. Another field trip was to Manchuria where Puyi met a peasant woman who had survived a mass execution by the Japanese. "Her amazing forgiveness," he wrote, "struck the Japanese war criminals dumb for a while, and then they began to weep for shame and kneel before her, asking the Chinese Government to punish them."

Young Mao Zedong and Chinese posters from the 1950s. The Five-star Red Flag was adopted by the People's Republic of China in 1949.

A photo of Puyi at the re-education camp; vintage Chinese posters promoting industrial development. The poster on the right features Mao Zedong.

Over the years, the "re-education" worked and Puyi became a sincere supporter of the ideas and policies of the Chinese Communist Party. But, just like in his days of being a puppet emperor, his access to news was severely limited. Between 1958 and 1962 the Chinese Communist Party embarked on a campaign of "industrialization" – called the **Great Leap Forward**. The campaign was badly mismanaged. So many people left farms to do construction projects and work at factories, that agricultural produce was not harvested. Famine followed. Millions starved to death. Another disastrous policy, the **Four Pests** campaign, contributed to this disaster. It directed farmers to kill sparrows (along with rats, mosquitoes, and flies) because sparrows steal grain from the fields. The population of sparrows fell so low that locusts and other insects (normally eaten by the sparrows) multiplied beyond control and devastated crops across China. The former emperor was clueless about these developments. His field trips were canceled to prevent him from seeing the horrors in the countryside.

9 years after Puyi returned from Russia, he was released from jail and was allowed to come to Beijing. Since the socialist system required all citizens of China to work, Puyi worked too – as a gardener at the Beijing Botanical Garden. He visited the Forbidden City palaces as a tourist and was amazed to see many things he had owned and used as a kid. Puyi re-married and lived as a common Chinese citizen until his death, in 1967.

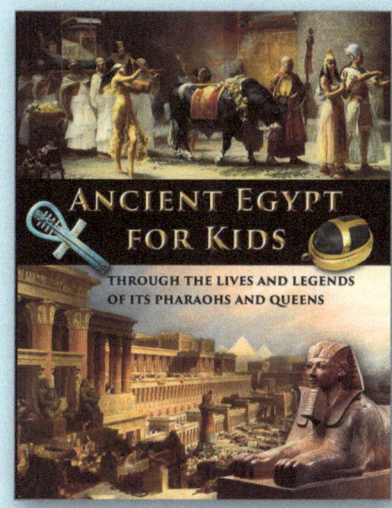
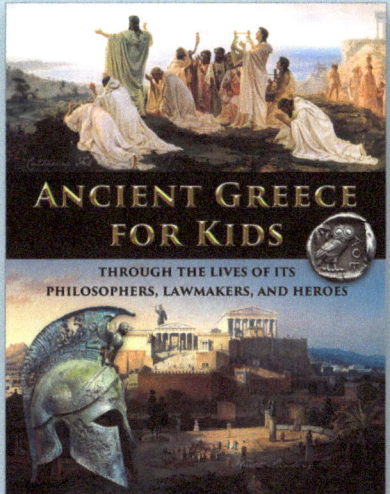
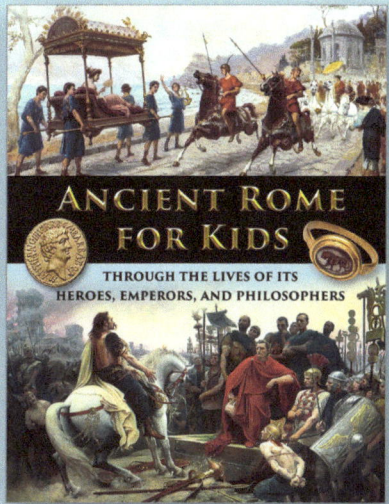
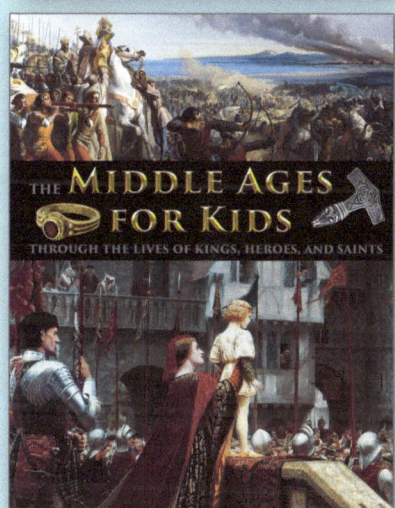
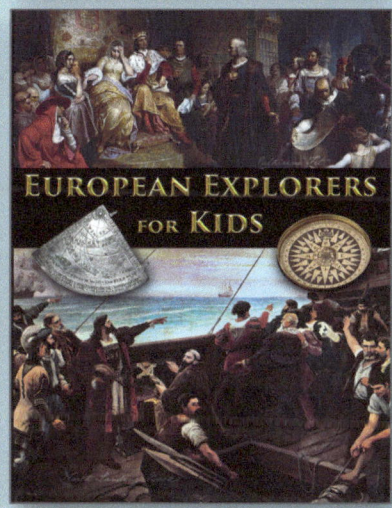
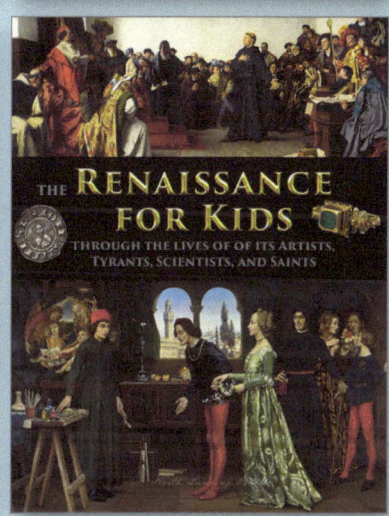
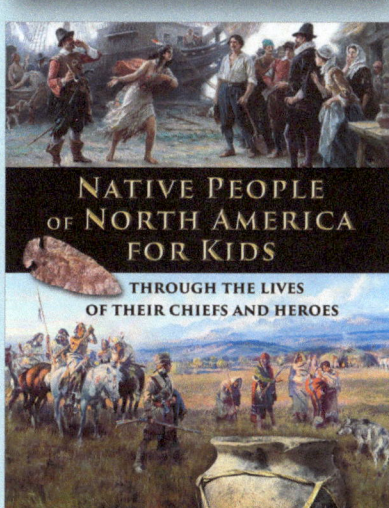
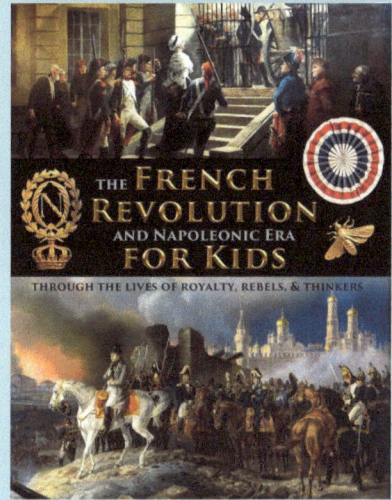
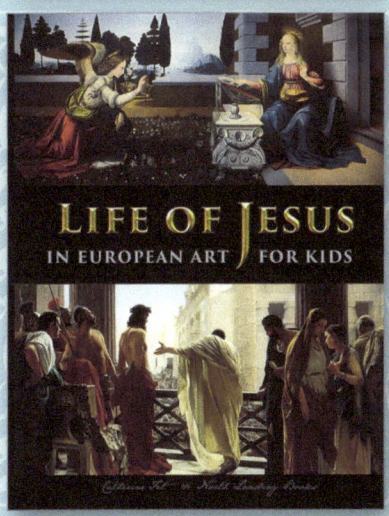

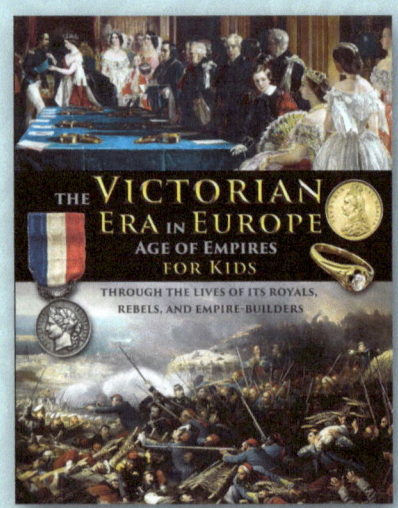
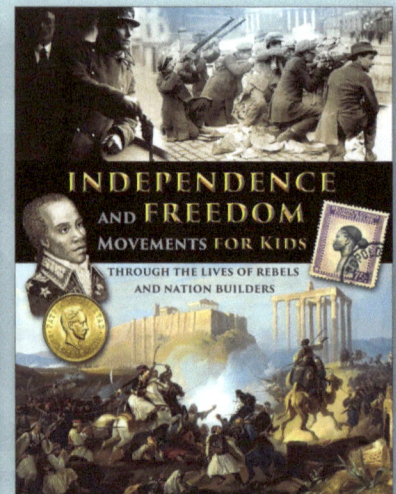
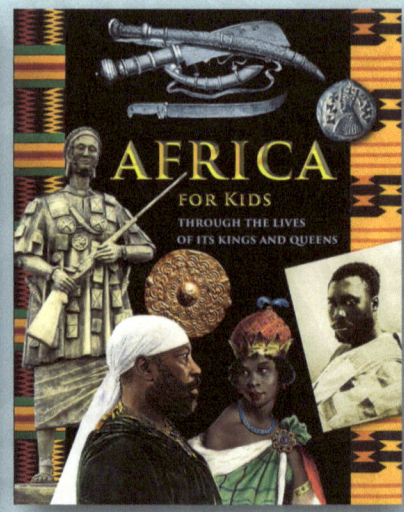
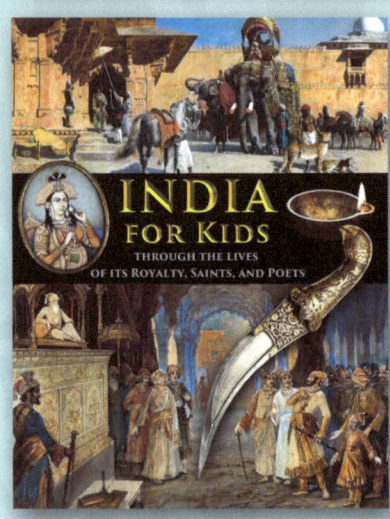
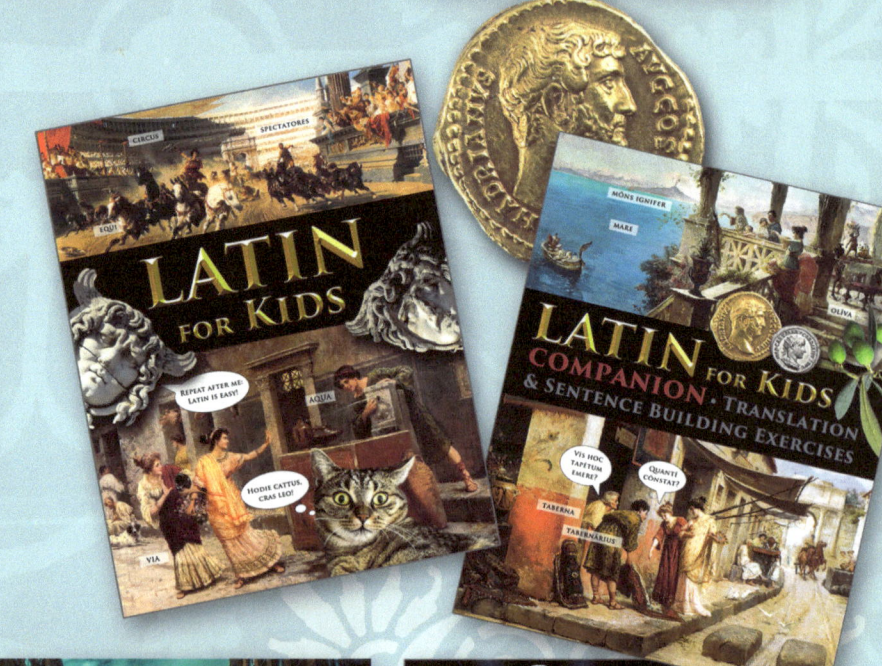
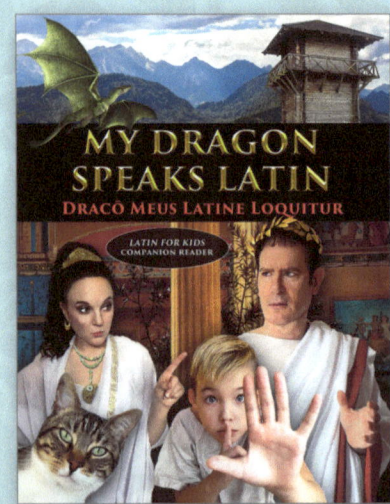

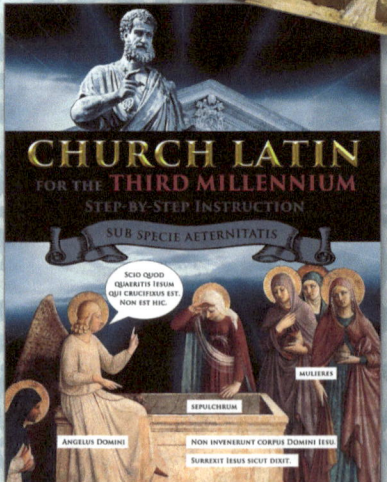